AF324273

ON THE SHOULDERS of a GIANT

by

Marion R. Cody

&

Doris I. Walker

QUIXOTE PRESS

Quixote Press
31798 K18S
Sioux City, IA
51109
1-800-571-BOOK

TABLE OF CONTENTS

RECOMMENDED READING

Encyclopedia of the Midwest by Allan Carpenter

Illinois by Robert P. Howard

Life on the Mississippi by Mark Twain

River Boats of America by Frank Donovan

INTRODUCTION

The very early northern Indians called the Mississippi River Messipi or Mechasipi, which translated into "Great River" or "Big River." Downstream civilization later dubbed it Old Man River, Father of Waters and the Mighty Mississippi.

It ranks as the third longest river in the world. It begins just below the Canadian border, and ends at the Gulf of Mexico. Its 2,470-mile length drains 1,225,000 square miles reaching eastward to within 250 miles of the Atlantic Ocean, and westward to within 500 miles of the Pacific. Its 40 tributaries flow from 31 states. All are at least partially navigable, creating 15,000 miles of inland waterways. The alluvial deposits of the Mississippi are the most fertile in the country, and its valley can feed and clothe the entire continent.

The Great River Road, the world's longest parkway, is the Mississippi's inseparable companion. From Canada to the Gulf, the road clings to the river like a shadow.

Mark Twain once wrote, "The Mississippi River towns are comely, clean, well built, pleasing to the eye, and cheering to the spirit." They are indeed, plus these communities are the very heart and soul of our country's development.

The Great Flood of '93 stunned the nation and tested the patience and fortitude of those living along the Mississippi between St. Paul. Minnesota and Cairo, Illinois. One hundred rivers, draining the rain-soaked Heartland and Crossroads sections of America, poured into the Mississippi during one of the wettest periods in history. Their impact is almost beyond measure. Uncontrolled water caused billions of dollars in destruction and took 45 lives. Almost every river community sustained some loss.

Although river people respect the power of a flooding river and accept the river's right to periodically reclaim its own land, they won't give in without a fight. Up and down the Mississippi, men, women, and children worked side by side, around the clock, filling and stacking sandbags used to control the raging water.

The Flood of '93 is gone now . . . but, as always, the river remains. Like a giant, it has its way.

. . . . **THE MISSISSIPPI RIVER** . . . . its highways and by-ways, its wide expanses and its secret little places . . . .

. . . . from Lake Itasca to the Deep Delta, this odyssey-in-a-book looks at the people, the places, and the life of that giant here in the middle of America.

QUIXOTE PRESS

Let us always remember the
folks who battled the flood
of 1993. Some won, and some
lost . . . . . . but they were
all winners.

Chapter One

IN THE BEGINNING

Dakota and Ojibwa Indians were the only inhabitants of northern Minnesota Territory until the late 1600s. This far-north section of the Mississippi Valley was their home and hunting grounds. The Algonquian-speaking Ojibwa called the river Messipi.

Father Louis Hennepin explored some of the area in 1680, which paved the way for French explorers, fur trappers,and traders. Most of the explorers were specifically looking for the fabled Northwest Passage to the Pacific Ocean.

The wilderness of the north was probably the world's richest source of fur-bearing animals. Mink, ermine, marten, muskrat, lynx, bear, wolverine, and beaver. The most prized was the beaver, not for its pelt, but for its woolly underfur. This material was used to make thick, firm hats for European men and women.

The million-dollar fur business was controlled by the English-owned Hudson's Bay Company, and North West Company, owned by the French. They were both based in Canada and were bitter rivals until their merger in 1821. The two operated very differently. Hudson's Bay employed the English boatmen and used wooden rowboats up to 40 feet in length. These boats worked very well on large rivers and lakes. The North West Company hired the colorful French-Canadians, known as voyageurs. These hearty men traveled on foot and paddled loaded canoes the 3,000-mile route from Montreal to Lake Athabasca. Made of birch-bark, on a light cedar frame, the canoes were suitable for swift water and light enough for portaging.

Because the 3,000 miles had to be covered in the five months between May and October, the route was divided into two legs, each traveled by a separate crew of voyageurs. One group paddled the 1,000 miles from Montreal to Grand Portage. Their canoes were loaded with 90-pound bales of goods to be traded with the Indians. The other crew traveled from Lake Athabasca to Grand Portage. Their canoes were all loaded with 90-pound bales of furs. They met in mid-July to exchange cargoes. Grand Portage was, and still is, the home of the Chippewa (Ojibwa) Indians. Many voyageurs took Indian wives.

The 1803 Louisiana Purchase opened the way for American exploration. A year later, the boundary between Canada and the United States was approved. American explorers were all military officers assigned to the United States Army Corps of Engineers. The Corps began in the American Revolution, with the construction of battlements at the Battle of Bunker Hill.

West Point Military Academy was established in 1802,to train officers in engineering skills essential to defense. The Corps constructed the Washington Monument, our Capitol Building, bridges

for all wars,the Panama Canal,the Alaskan Highway,
and surveyed the Trans-Continental Railway. They
have also improved over 29,000 miles of water routes
on the Tennessee, Cumberland, Ohio, Illinois,
Missouri, Arkansas,and Mississippi rivers.They are
known as the American Builders. The Corps' work
continues today.

Meriwether Lewis, William Clark, Zebulon Pike,
Henry Shreve, Stephen Long, and John Fremont were
officers assigned to the exploration unit, called
the Corps of Discovery.They explored,surveyed,and
mapped all of America's vast land west of the
Mississippi River. Their wise efforts safeguarded
many of our natural wonders,such as Yellowstone and
Sequoia, from exploitation

In 1805, Zebulon Pike was sent from St,Louis to
find the headwaters of the Mississippi River.
Although he never found the source, his maps were
invaluable to those who followed. That same year,
Meriwether Lewis and William Clark had traced the
Missouri River and had reached the mouth of the
Columbia River. Opening this new land enabled Jacob
Astor to establish his American Fur Company.

By 1820,the land between New Orleans, Louisiana, and St. Louis, Missouri, was lined with early settlements and New Orleans had developed into an important shipping center. Settlers had not yet ventured into the Mississippi Valley above St.Louis, but northern white pine was perfect for building southern homes. Its popularity eventually spread throughout the entire nation, and a new industry was born. Lumbering reigned for almost a century.

Logging began as a crude operation. It required agility and brute strength. Trees were cut in the winter and sledded to frozen river tributaries. With the coming of the spring thaw, logs were pushed into the water and floated downstream to a boom (barrier) on or near the Mississippi River. Lumberjacks then sorted, branded, and formed the logs into rafts, which were floated down the river. Upon reaching their destination, usually New Orleans, the rafts were sold and logging crews booked passage on the next northbound steamboat.

Timber thefts were general by 1860. Logging camps were set up with no evidence of ownership. A more subtle technique of acquiring large stands of pine was accomplished by obtaining tracts of land granted to returning Civil War veterans. Another method was to obtain a government grant for something such as a road or a railroad, thereby acquiring a wide swath through the forest.

Frederick Weyerhauser, a German businessman, came to America at the age of 22. After working for lumber companies in Pennsylvania and Illinois, he moved to St.Paul, Minnesota, and formed the Mississippi Logging Company.

Early timber rafts were simple, but by 1880, all rafting methods were improved and steam power was utilized. Irish immigrants devised a way to rig a raft so it could be pushed with a towboat. Not only did this mean a faster trip downriver, it meant the raft size could be increased from feet of lumber to acres of lumber. Towboat captains dealt directly with lumber camps. The boat crew consisted of a pilot and a few roustabouts, called "roosters." It was no simple task to guide the huge rafts down the dangerous Mississippi.

The great lumber industry ended as suddenly as it began. The vast white pine forests of the north were gone and only barren wasteland remained by the year 1915.

Reforestation is an ongoing process in the north. Mississippi Valley forests appear young and sparse. Most are now being used for the manufacture of paper products.

Chapter Two

THE FAR NORTH

Minnesota's Lake Itasca, the cradle of the Mississippi River, was well-known to Indians and traders. The Indians called it Omushkos. French traders called it Lac la Viche, both names meant "elk or red deer lake."

Explorer Henry Schoolcraft visited this northern Minnesota area in 1832. He became friendly with the Indians and told them of his search for the headwaters of the Mississippi. They took him to Omushkos, which he later renamed Itasca, Latin meaning "truth and head."

Schoolcraft's famous legend tells of the mythical Ojibwa Chief Hiawatha and his daughter, Itasca.

Itasca was stolen by the ruler of the spirits of the dead to be his bride and live in the dark underworld. Her tears, shed in sadness for the world she would leave behind, flowed together forming Lake Itasca.

The lake has three arms: East, West, and North. The Mississippi flows from the north end of the North Arm as a gentle stream about 12 feet in width. One can wade the shallow river or use the stepping stones placed between the banks. One can also cross the river on a narrow bridge, the first of many spans across the Mississippi, as well as the smallest.

Although temperatures sometimes reach as low as 40° below zero in winter, the headwaters rarely freeze over. Springs feed enough water into the lake to continue its flow. The river's surface speed is 1.2 miles per hour. A raindrop on the lake would arrive at the Gulf of Mexico in about ninety days, if it didn't evaporate.

The headwaters area, set aside as Minnesota's first state park in 1891, preserves 32,000 acres of woods and lakes.

As the river flows north and east toward more populated regions, it arrives at our nation's first Mississippi River Main Street, Bemidji, Minnesota.The city is named for an Indian Chief whose name meant "easy crossing." Although a few visitors came in 1866, its main settlement began 20 years later, as the Carson Trading Post. The arrival of railroads helped launch Bemidji's development as a lumbering center. Bemidji Woolen Mills located here in 1921.

Bemidji has a current population of around 11,000. It is situated on a strip of land between Lake Irving and the larger Lake Bemidji. The giant lumberjack of American folklore is honored here. Huge colorful statues of Paul Bunyan and his blue ox, Babe, watch over Lake Bemidji.

Paul Bunyan stories probably originated in early lumber camps. Several tales involved Johnny Inkslinger and Shot Gunderson, his loggong crew. Others were of his blue ox, Babe, ("twice as big as all outdoors and playful as a hurricane"), and her tremendous appetite for hay and potato peels, and her ability to haul a whole forest of logs. One story told of Babe's great thirst and how Paul had to scoop out the Great Lakes to provide enough drinking water for her. Another described when Babe needed new shoes how Big Ole, the blacksmith, had to open a new iron mine in Minnesota. Still other tales were of Paul Bunyan himself. One traces his career from infancy, when he stepped out of his cradle and caused a 70-foot tide in Canada's Bay of Fundy. Another classic concerns his pancake griddle, which was so large skaters had to tie sides of bacon to their shoes to grease it. Others incidents tell how Paul dug Puget Sound, in Washington, to float huge logs to the mill, when he hung his Big Dipper handy to the Milky Way,

and when he logged off the moon to open up the space age. Paul Bunyan tales followed a specific form. All were told matter-of-factly, as if by an eyewitness.

The chain of lakes around Bemidji was part of a major route used by early explorers. It was known as Red Lake Trail and connected Leech Lake and Red Lake.

An interesting north woods sight, in early spring, is tapping of sap from sugar bush maples.

The small communities of Cass Lake, Bena, Ball Club, and Deer River are located along the river between Bemidji and Grand Rapids. All of them played an important role in the early lumbering industry.

At Grand Rapids, the Mississippi abruptly turns south. Three-mile-long rapids prompted Indians to call the area "long rapids." The town's growth began around the Northwest Trading Post. In the late 1800s, lumber milling became the leading industry. the

rapids provided more than enough power to run the mills. Grand Rapids was also the northernmost riverport for steamboats coming upriver from the Minneapolis area. Although logging declined in the early 1900s, paper manufacturing continues today. The Forest History Center provides an excellent opportunity to experience life in an early lumber camp. Minnesota's longest and wildest groomed snowmobile trail begins at Grand Rapids and extends 170 miles northeast, to Ely, Minnesota. The city is also the gateway to the Mesabi Iron Range. Its current population is nearly 8,000.

After leaving Grand Rapids, the Mississippi passes through Aitkin, Minnesota, an early-day riverboat center and Brainerd, an important shipping point.

Brainerd was established in 1860, when the railroad was built across the Mississippi. Today's population numbers over 11,000.

Below Brainerd is Little Falls, where lumbering became a big business when the area's first dam was built in 1849. The dam provided power for a sawmill . Flour milling began in the middle 1850s. The mansions of lumber barons Charles Weyerhauser and R. D. Musser are on display there. Lindbergh State Park, on the banks of the Mississippi, surrounds the boyhood home of Charles A. Lindbergh.

Downriver, St. Cloud, Minnesota, a city of 45,000, began in 1853 as three separate settlements, started by three different men. One was interested in fur trading, one wanted a sawmill, and one was a developer. The settlements merged in 1856 and became St.Cloud, named for Napolean's residence at St. Cloud, France, near Paris. The community was an important crossroad for river traffic and ox carts routes to the forts and settlements in the Red River Valley. Colorful granite deposits were discovered nearby, in 1868.

Father Louis Hennepin discovered and named the Falls of St. Anthony in 1680. They are the only falls on the entire Mississippi River and were sacred to the Indians.

Minneapolis began with fur trading. Its name is a combination of minne, which is Indian meaning "water" and polis, which is Greek meaning "city." Henry Sibley's home, below the Falls of St. Anthony, was constructed in 1835, and served as the headquarters of the American Fur Company.

In Mark Twain's account of his 1882 steamboat trip from New Orleans to St. Paul, Minnesota, he described St. Anthony Falls as "stretching across the river 1,500 feet and with a fall of 82 feet." He also stated that "Minneapolis had 30 flour mills, 20 sawmills, woolen and paper mills, and other factories. Flour mills used the *new process* of mashing the wheat by rolling instead of grinding."

The devastating flour mill explosions, in 1878, destroyed half of the milling industry. Nevertheless, the Pillsbury "A" Mills, at the falls, was completed in 1881, and by 1905 claimed to be the world's largest flour mill. Pillsbury's agricultural interests continued to grow and expand.

Minnesota has two popular giants today. Paul Bunyan , lumberjack of the north, and Pillsbury's "Green Giant," jolly master of the southern vegetable fields. His "ho, ho, ho," is recognized by all.

Minneapolis is considered to be one of the nation's most liveable cities and has a current population of around 400,000.

Around 1820, the government constructed Fort St. Anthony, which was later renamed Fort Snelling. It was located at the confluence of the Minnesota and Mississippi rivers. After a perilous journey the first steamboat, the Virginia, reached the fort in 1823, carrying supplies and passengers.

The shallowness of the Mississippi River above St. Louis, Missouri, the dangerous lower rapids at Keokuk, Iowa, and the even more dangerous upper rapids at Rock Island, Illinois, made steamboat travel nearly impossible on the Upper Mississippi. Congress began to address these problems as early as 1824 when the United States Army Corps of Engineers was assigned to eliminate both rapids areas and maintain a channel 4 feet in depth.

Forty-two years of charts, surveys, and reports, along with the Civil War followed. There seemed to be little hope at all for improving the upper rapids. One project supervisor estimated that it would take "forever."

Serious work began when new equipment and the steam-powered chisel was introduced in 1866. By that time , a lateral canal with three locks had been built along the west bank of the river, which bypassed the lower rapids, at Keokuk. Twenty years later, in

1886, a 4-foot channel was finally completed on the upper rapids, but even before it was finished, increased river traffic and larger boats had rendered it obsolete.

The next 20 years saw a sharp decline in all types of river traffic. Railroads thrived and took over most of the river shipping. In order to compete, a 6-foot depth would be needed to accomodate larger boats with barges. Congress authorized this improvement.

By 1913, Hamilton Water Power Company had replaced Keokuk's lateral canal and locks with a power dam across the Mississippi and a single lock, whose operation they turned over to the Corps of Engineers. The new lock and dam inundated the entire lower rapids and its canal.

The extreme upper section of the crooked Rock Island rapids was to be bypassed by a canal and lock at Le Claire, Iowa. World War I interrupted this project, but a lock 320 feet long and 80 feet wide opened in November 1922.

During World War I, the War Department's Federal Barge Lines had proven that it was cheaper to ship goods by river than by railroad, and were pleading for better river navigation. Strong pressures came for a new 9-foot channel depth. This monumental project was authorized in 1930, and work began in 1931. With the lock and dam at Keokuk already in place, the 1930 Act called for 25 new locks and dams. It also provided for a uniform lock size of 110 feet wide and 600 feet long, the same as had been

established for the Ohio River. By 1940, the entire
project was completed, thereby creating a 650-mile
stairway of controlled lakes, enabling the river to

be maintained at a constant 9-foot depth. During the
spring thaw, when water is plentiful, all gates are
opened and the Mississippi becomes a free-flowing
river.

Lock and Dam No. 1 is located above Fort Snelling,
just before Minnehaha Creek plunges 53 feet into the
Mississippi. Minnehaha Falls is a popular spot along
the river and a bronze statue of Hiawatha and his
bride, Minnehaha, stands at the top of the falls.

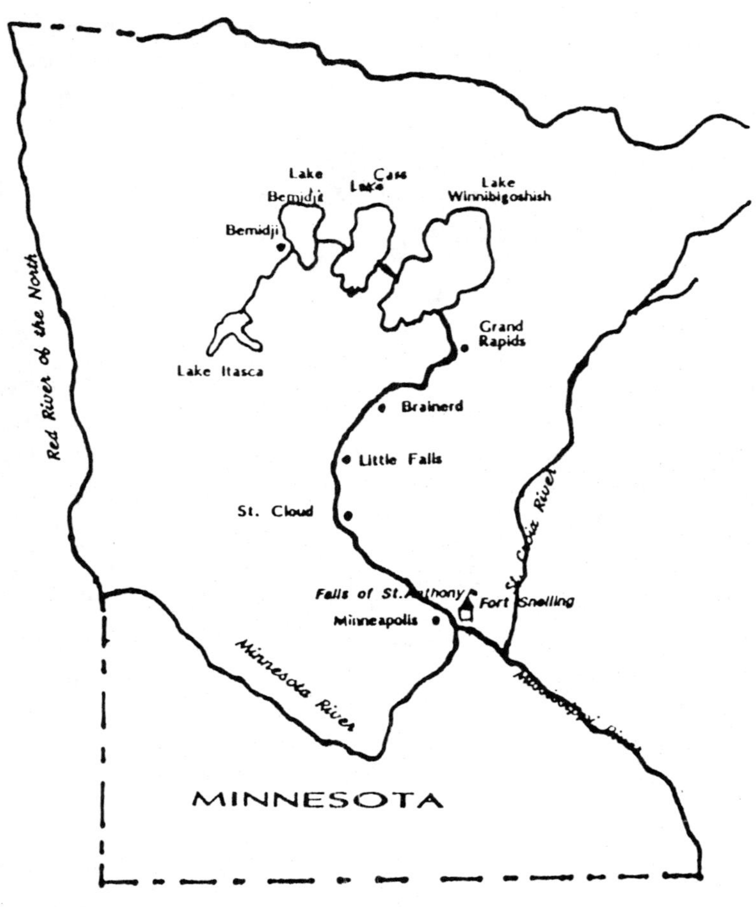

The Far North

Chapter Three

AMERICA'S HEARTLAND

The heartland section of the Mississippi River begins at St. Paul. Minnesota, and extends south to just above St. Louis, Missouri.

With the coming of the steamboat, St. Paul was destined to grow rapidly. Because of St. Anthony Falls, all river shipments going to the Upper Midwest had to be unloaded and transferred to ox cart to continue to their final destinations. Regular steamboat service was established in 1847.

The city's first beginnings were in 1838 when whiskey trader, Pierre Parrant, settled there. The area was given his unpleasing nickname, which was Pig's Eye. The community was spared however, when a log cabin chapel was built in 1841, and dedicated as St. Paul. Residents quickly responded and changed the settlement's name to match. The first store opened in 1842, and a town was platted in 1846.

Minnesota is a name of Indian origin, meaning "sky-tinted water." The state joined the Union in 1858, and is known as the Gopher State. St. Paul was chosen to be its capital and developed into a very important center for government and trade. The State Capitol Building was completed in 1904. Many historic buildings remain for public viewing. Minneapolis and St. Paul, known as the Twin Cities, are rich in history and culture.

Leaving St. Paul, the Mississippi River flows southeast. After wrapping itself around Grey Cloud Island, it passes through Lock and Dam No. 2. This lock is a 600-foot structure capable of lifting and lowering boats 12 feet. This is a very busy lock.

Hastings, Minnesota, began in 1831 as a wheat farming community. The actual settlement started as Olivers Grove in 1850, and was renamed Hastings in 1853. It is said to be the site of Minnesota's first flour mill, which was built in 1857. Just south of Hastings is the Mississippi's largest island, called Prairie Island.

Prescott, Wisconsin, lies across the bridge at Hastings, and for the first time, Minnesota must share the Mississippi River with another state.

Jean Nicolet explored some of Wisconsin in 1634. Trapping became the area's prominent early-day industry. By 1818 Jacob Astor's American Fur Company was in control of the region's fur business.

Like the rest of the land around the Great Lakes, Wisconsin was heavily forested and water was plentiful. Many of its rivers drain into the Mississippi. The Wisconsin River, which is 430 miles long, St. Croix, Rock River, and Chippewa all add large volumes of water to the Mississippi.
Wisconsin is known as the Badger State and was admitted into the Union in 1848. Its name is Ojibwa, meaning "gathering of waters."

Prescott, an attractive river town of 2,000 people, sits on the east bank of the beautiful St. Croix River.

Back on the Minnesota side of the Mississippi, Red Wing, a city of about 14,000, is located just below Lock and Dam No. 3. If you cross the bridge here, you will notice the river has separated into two wide channels. One is designated as the Wisconsin Mississippi River Channel, the other as the Minnesota Mississippi River Channel.

Red Wing was an Indian village as early as 1836, and was named for an old Sioux Chief, known as "wing of scarlet," which also meant "wing of the wild swan

dyed scarlet." American settlement began with the establishment of a steamboat port around 1850, making Red Wing one of Minnesota's oldest towns. It was an early stopping point for travelers.

After leaving Red Wing, the Mississippi expands to a two-mile width forming the gorgeous Lake Pepin. The lake is about 22 miles long and subject to violent storms with waves reaching heights up to 20 feet. Lake Pepin suppodrted a large clamming industry in the early 1900s. It is also the place where Ralph Samuelson, in 1922, invented water skis.

Lake City, Minnesota, population 4,500, enjoys a beautiful view of Lake Pepin from the west bank. The Wisconsin community of Pepin, population nearing 900, occupies the east bank. This area was the birthplace of Laura Ingalls Wilder who authored the

"Little House Books." Two miles south of Pepin, the Chippewa River joins the Mississippi. A dam of silt has been deposited in the Mississippi by this meeting. The very earliest settlement here dates back to 1686 and Fort Antoine.

The nearest bridge crossing the Mississippi, is another 14 miles downriver, at Nelson, very near the Chippewa-Mississippi confluence. With a small population of 400, Nelson is the home of a five-generation, family operated cheese factory. It will be difficult to pass by without sampling.

The small village of Alma, Wisconsin, is about nine miles south. It is located on a narrow strip of land between the Mississippi River and 500-foot bluffs. The town is only two blocks wide, but over seven miles long. Lock and Dam No. 4 sits within the town limits.

The bridge near Nelson leads to the west bank of the Mississippi and Wabasha, Minnesota. This is an interesting town of 2,400 friendly people. It is one of the oldest towns in the state. Established in 1830, it was named for the Sioux Chief Wag-pa-sha. The Anderson House is said to be Minnesota's oldest continuously operated hotel. It opened for business in 1856. Its rooms are furnished with antique items. It is popular for its Dutch cuisine. Wabasha has constructed the Eagle Watch Observatory down by the river. The eagle population declined with the use of DDT (caused thin eggshells), but with the ban, the population is now recovering. The observatory operates November through March.

Downriver, a huge bluff called Sugar Loaf, marks the entrance to Winona, Minnesota. The town began in the logging days of the 1800s, and was named for the beautiful Sioux Princess, Wenonah. Early settlers knew the town as an important riverport and railroad center for lumber and wheat shipments. Winona had two button factories in the early 1900s. Pearl buttons were made from clams taken from Lake Pepin. The city of 25,000 is the home of the Wilkie Steamboat Museum. Locks and Dams Nos, 5 and 5A are located just above Winona. Lock and Dam No. 6 is situated ten miles below.

La Crescent is Minnesota's last major river crossing. The town sits below forested limestone

bluffs. It is referred to as the "Apple Capital" of
Minnesota. Two bridges cross the Mississippi here.
Both lead to La Crosse, Wisconsin.

La Crosse began as a trading post in the 1700s and
saw its first log cabin
in 1842. It was named for the
Indian game of lacrosse. It is
a very modern agricultural and
industrial city with a total
population exceeding 48,000. It is squeezed between
Grandad Bluff and the Black River, where the Black
meets the Mississippi.

Cranberries are said to be Wisconsin's number one
fruit crop. The small town of Warrens, about 60 miles
east of La Crosse, is the "Cranberry Capital" of the
state. The Cranberry Expo Ltd.,complete with museum,
sits on a nearby family-owned cranberry marsh. It is
open to anyone interested in the industry.

Wisconsin's original section of the Great River
Road was constructed and dedicated in 1952. The state
marker is located a few miles north of La Crosse.

Lock and Dam No. 8, Minnesota's last, is about 15 miles downriver. The Mississippi has traveled over 600 miles through its birth state. It has moved through peaceful woods, bustling cities, and flat productive farmlands. It now becomes Iowa's eastern boundary.

Iowa is an Indian word meaning "beautiful land." The state was named for its earliest inhabitants, the Ioway Indians.

Small bands of Sac and Fox wandered down from Wisconsin in the 1700s, but in general, Iowa had very few Indians prior to the Louisiana Purchase. As settlers pushed westward, other tribes arrived. Potawotomi, Winnebago, and Sioux all played important roles in Iowa's early history.

Iowa came into the Union in 1846 and is called the Hawkeye State. It is a land of tall corn, and contains one-quarter of the nation's prime farmland. It is also industrial. One hundred twenty-five of the top five hundred manufacturers have plant sites within

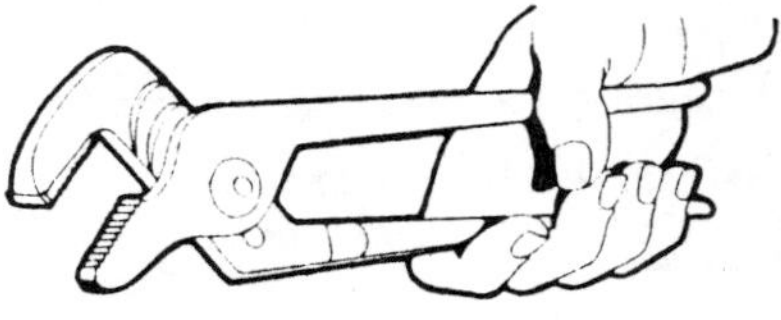

the state. The Mississippi River plays a large role in shipping Iowa commodities.

The northeastern region of the state is quite often referred to as "Switzerland Of Iowa." Beautiful rolling hills and towering limestone bluffs follow the Mississippi along most of Iowa's east boundary.

Lansing is Iowa's northernmost river town. The bridge, across the Mississippi, leads to a sportsman's paradise near Ferryville, Wisconsin. In addition to hunting and fishing, the town is noted for its Ferryville Cheese Factory.

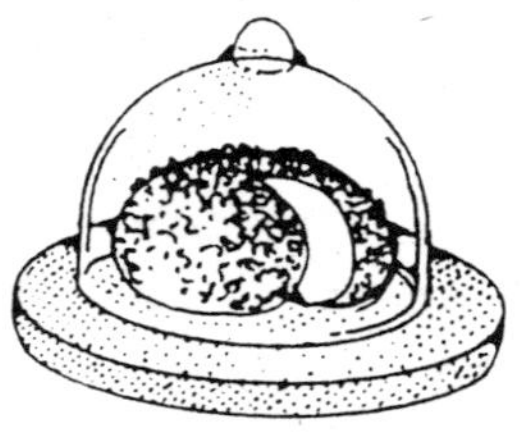

Lock and Dam No. 9 straddles the river between Lansing and Harper's Ferry. This is the first of 11 structures along the Iowa boundary.

Effigy Mounds, Iowa's only National Monument, is located another 12 miles to the south. The Monument sets apart 191 pre-historic Indian burial mounds built in the shapes of birds and animals. The mounds are estimated to be 2,500 years old.

The adjoining villages of Marquette and McGregor are just outside the park. The bluff overlooking the river here, is the site of Pikes Peak State Park. When Zebulon Pike made his expedition up the Mississippi, the army asked him to look for suitable sites for constructing a fort along the west bank of the river.

This bluff was one of his choices. McGregor was the home of a German harness maker whose sons founded the great Ringling Brothers Circus.

Prairie du Chien, a larger town of 5,900, lies across the Mississippi River Bridge in Wisconsin. Its name means "prairie of the dog" , which in turn,

refers to an Indian Chief named Alim, meaning "dog." In the early times of exploration, this was the final destination for all who came by way of the Great Lakes. Their trip required them to paddle the Fox River, then portage over to the Wisconsin River, where they would drift down to the Mississippi. Prairie du Chien is Wisconsin's second-oldest settlement, dating back to 1685, when Nicolas Perrot was sent to establish a fort at the mouth of the Wisconsin.
One of the popular attractions here is the Villa Louis Mansion. This beautiful home was built in the 1870s by Wisconsin's first millionaire, Hercules Douseman.

The Wisconsin River joins the Missisippi just south of town. Marquette and Jolliet entered the Mississippi here in 1673 on their most famous float trip. From the towering gray bluff above, at

Wyalusing State Park, one gets a birds-eye view of both rivers. This view, enclosed by gray bluffs topped with large trees and dense foliage, is beautiful any time of the year.

Guttenberg, Iowa, is reached by crossing back to the west bank of the Mississippi and continuing downriver. Lock and Dam No. 10 sits in the middle of town and an excellent view is made possible by a mile-long city park bordering the lock. Guttenberg's population exceeds 2,400. Many historic buildings have been preserved and a copy of the Guttenberg Bible is displayed at the local newspaper office.

The small community of Millville, Iowa, is located about six miles south, where the Turkey River flows into the Mississippi. A well-marked road out of Millville, leads to a rare opportunity on the Upper Mississippi. The Cassville Car Ferry, one of the few still in service, operates between Millville and Cassville, Wisconsin. It accomodates everything from walk-on passengers to semis and tour buses, and operates from May to November.

Cassville is a town of about 1,300 people. Nearby,
is the Nelson Dewey State
Park and Stonefield Village, a
reconstructed replica of an 1890s
rural community.

Lock and Dam No. 11 sits about 20 miles below
Cassville, near the Wisconsin-Illinois-Iowa
boundary. It is Wisconsin's last river structure. By
the time the Mississippi reaches this area, it has
followed approximately 250 miles of Wisconsin's West
Coast.

This tristate area is where Mississippi River
commerce began. When rich lead deposits were found
here, in the late 1700s and early 1800s, early
shipments were floated downstream on rafts and crude
barges.

THE STEAMBOAT ERA

Robert Fulton's boat the New Orleans, was the
first steamboat on the Mississippi. It left
Pittsburg. Pennsylvania, in September 1811, and
arrived at New Orleans January 1812, after picking up
a small load of cotton at Natchez, Mississippi. His
boat withstood the terrible New Madrid earthquakes
of 1811 and 1812 which shook the Mississippi

Valley and completely altered the course of the river. Fulton's steamboats were designed for deep water. They were not suitable for the shallow waters of the Mississippi.

Henry Shreve, for whom Shreveport, Louisiana is named, built his first boat, called a keelboat, in 1807, the same year Fulton built his steamboat.Shreve's keelboat carried cargo from Pittsburg, down the Ohio, then up the Mississippi to St. Louis, Missouri. He later returned to continue upriver to the lead mines at Galena, Illinois. The flat-bottom design of the keelboat allowed it to ride on, not in, the water. It was also more able to navigate rapids.

For the next decade, barges, rafts, and keelboats  continued to float shipments downstream, but had to be poled or sailed upstream. Trips took many months.

Based on his keelboat design, Shreve finished his first Mississippi River steamboat in 1816, which he named the Washington. It was the prototype for all future steamboats on the river.

With the coming of steam power, goods could be shipped anywhere on the river. Downriver shipments continued to be floated on rafts and keelboats, and steamboats now carried shipments upriver.

The boat's bells and whistles were the most prized of all possessions. Bells started as a means of signaling workers when landing or departing. Whistles were melodious. They were several-toned instruments keyed to be distinguishable. Some blew a chord, some a succession of different notes, and some blew both. It was hard to find two whistles alike. Combinations of long and short blasts signaled different situations. Many residents along the river were able to name the boat coming, long before it arrived.

The smallest steamboat used 30 cords of wood each day. Before farmers and settlers arrived, deckhands were forced to stop and cut wood twice daily. As towns

and farms were cleared, commercial woodlots were set up along the river. If the woodlot owner happened to be away, the steamboat crew loaded the wood and left payment, with a note.

The average life of early steamboats was less than three years. Many factors contributed to this: the river was busy and extremely crowded. Along with private travel and local use, heavily-loaded commercial rafts and barges still floated downriver. Any control their crews might have had, could be quickly erased by sudden adverse weather conditions or unexpectedly strong river currents;the course of the river could change overnight; underwater wreckage was a hazzard;devastating fires and boiler explosions were prevalent.

Almost nothing existed above St. Louis. Hannibal had only a smithy; a settler was clearing the land where Quincy, Illinois, would stand; Galena's lead mines were there; Dubuque, Iowa, was a group of deserted huts and the grave site of Julien Dubuque; there was no white civilization in Iowa or Minnesota; and a few Indian villages dotted the riverbank. Indians distrusted the steamboats and called them "fire canoes."

River pilot licenses were issued for specific stretches of the Mississippi. In the late 1850s, America's most famous river pilot, Mark Twain, held a

license to pilot between St.Louis, Missouri,and New Orleans, Louisiana.

Most steamboats are now diesel-powered. Two exceptions, the Delta Queen and the Mississippi Queen, are still steam-powered. The Delta Queen, a four-deck stern-wheeler, is 285 feet long. She was built in Scotland in 1926. The Mississippi Queen is the largest steamboat ever, 382 feet long. She is also a stern-wheeler and was commissioned in 1976. Their home port is New Orleans. They still make various trips on the Mississippi, Ohio, and Tennessee rivers.

Picturesque old steamboats would be no match for today's diesel-powered towboats. One of the largest cargoes ever carried by a river steamer was 9,226 bales of cotton, weighing 2,390 tons. Today. a tow of over 22,000 tons of freight, loaded on 12 or 15 barges, all pushed by one sturdy little towboat, is a common sight. It would require 58 semi trucks to carry the same tonnage. A typical barge is 35 feet wide, 195 feet long and carries 1,500 tons. A 15-barge tow is the usual size on the Upper Mississippi, which is 3 barges wide and 5 barges long. The barges are fastened together and pushed as a unit, by a towboat located at the rear, behind the middle barge. A maximum of 17 barges is allowed by locating one barge on either side of the towboat.The overall length is one-fourth mile. Great skill is required to steer a vessel this long, and it requires about five miles to get a tow stopped. The overall width is 105 feet and the unit must be steered through locks measuring only 110 feet in width.

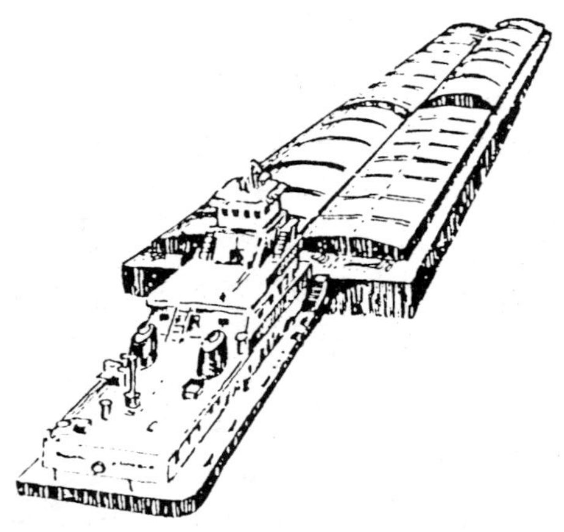

The conveniences of the towboat may surprise many old rivermen. Hydraulic steering, echo sounders, pneumatic hoists, air conditioning, refrigeration, television, radio-telephones, and radar are all standard equipment today. The boat holds almost 64,000 gallons of diesel fuel, enough for two weeks of travel. It also stores 14,000 gallons of fresh water.

A towboat carries a crew of 11, made up of the captain, pilot, chief engineer, engineer, mate, watchman, cook, and four deckhands. The crew lives together on the boat six months out of the year. They care for one another, as a family, and take great pride in their boat.

Members of the crew take two six-hour watches each day, with watches changing at 6 o'clock and at 12 o'clock. The cook serves meals one hour before and after each watch change. Crews work one-month shifts, and are replaced by new crews monthly. It requires about seven days for a tow to make the trip between St.Louis, Missouri, and St. Paul, Minnesota.

A new riverboat era began April 1, 1991, when the State of Iowa approved gaming on the river. Excitement along Iowa's eastern shore is almost reminiscent of Mark Twain days. Port cities are responding and riverfronts are coming alive. Old

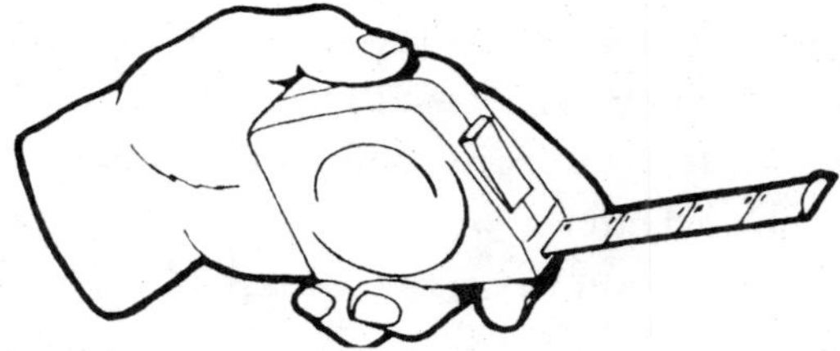

crumbling brick buildings are being replaced by new shops amd restaurants. Each city is working to preserve its unique river heritage.

These magnificent vessels are diesel-powered paddle wheelers. Their decks are painted and polished. Their Victorian interiors are simply elegant. Casinos, outfitted with the very latest electronic machines, fill complete decks. Other decks offer delicious dining, and observation decks are available for all. Most states, bordering the Mississippi, now have plans in progress concerning gaming on the river. There is no better way to see the river, than from the river. As you drift by the changing scenes, don't be surprised if a feeling of nostalgia creeps over you. After all, what you are seeing hasn't changed that much in the last century.

Dubuque, on the west side of Lock and Dam No. 11, is the oldest city in Iowa. It is also one of the largest, with a current population over 62,000. Its first inhabitants were Sac and Fox Indians. Marquette and Jolliet visited in 1673, but its first roots as a city, started with Julien Dubuque in 1788. He gained the trust and friendship of the Fox Indians and they granted him permission to work the nearby lead mines on both sides of the Mississippi River.

His fur trading and mining activities extended from
Prairie du Chien, Wisconsin, to St. Louis, Missouri.
When Zebulon Pike was sent to explore the Upper
Mississippi, he visited Dubuque's mines.

Like other towns along the river, lumbering became
a large industry. Sawmills were built to process logs
rafted down the river. Other industries sprang up
and by the mid 1800s, Dubuque's population had grown
to around 13,000. A steam ferry to Illinois began
operating to accomodate the lead miners, at Galena.
By 1870, Dubuque was connected to the eastern United
States by a railroad bridge.

Ice Harbor, made by building a floodwall, provided
a winter shelter for boats.
It was also a boat building
site. When Ice Harbor froze,
ice was cut and used in the
city's iceboxes.

One of the city's unique early-day structures was
the Fenelon Place Elevator, also called Fourth
Street Elevator. It claims to be the world's shortest
scenic railway, measuring 296 feet in length. It

lifts passengers from downtown Fourth Street, to Fenelon Place on the bluff, a height of 189 feet. It was built by J. K. Graves, a local banker, who commuted between downtown and his residence on the bluff. The distance was less than three blocks, but the round-trip by horse and buggy, took an hour. He decided a cable car would shorten his travel time. He promptly petitioned the city for the right to build. Permission was granted and his project was completed in 1882.

Dubuque produced lead shot during the Civil War. Old Shot Tower still stands on Fourth Street, at the river. Eagle Point Park sits high on a bluff overlooking Lock and Dam No,11. The dam is over 4,800 feet in length. It was completed in 1937, and named the General Zebulon Pike Lock and Dam. Trolley tours,carriage rides, river excursions, and river gaming are all available at Ice Harbor.

Nearby Dyersville, Iowa calls itself the farm

toy capital of the world. It
offers displays of Ertl's most
authentic replicas of farm

machinery. Also at Dyersville, is the 1988 "Field of
Dreams" movie site. If you saw the movie, you will
surely recognize the baseball diamond among the
cornfields.

Dubuque has two Mississippi River bridges. The
Highway 61 bridge goes back into Wisconsin. The
Julien Dubuque Bridge, Highway 20, goes to East
Dubuque, Illinois.

Illinois was the western border for the United
States until the Louisiana Purchase placed it in the
center of the nation. Illinois was named for the
Illinwek Indians. It is known as the Prairie State
and joined the Union in 1818.

The famous village of Galena, one
of Illinois' earliest settlements,
is located 15 miles south of East
Dubuque, Under an 1823 leasing system,
thousands of settlers rushed to this
area of rich lead deposits. While many
worked the mines, many others chose to build stores
and businesses. The town is located where the Galena
River flows into the Mississippi, and during its most

active days, Galena was the largest riverport
between St.Louis and St.Paul. It recorded over 100
steamboat arrivals each day. It also was the final
stop for the old Frink and Walker Stage. This line

brought many settlers from the East. The stage
originated in Chicago, and the trip to Galena took
five days, if all went well. Galena was a bustling
boomtown by 1830, and incorporated in 1839.

Nothing could hold the miners in Galena when gold
was discovered in California. They left as quickly as
they came. Most of the settlers who remained, went
back to the land. By the mid 1800s, agriculture was
Galena's dominant industry. Many of the town's
permanent buildings were constructed at that time.
Among them is the DeSota Hotel, where Abraham Lincoln
once spoke, and the United States Custom House Post
Office. Most of Galena is now listed on the National
Register of Historic Places. Most of downtown
buildings and historic hotels are open to the

Galena was a favorite retirement place for Civil War generals. Ulysses S. Grant's family lived there before the war. A brick home was presented to him when he returned from active duty. The town was the home of nine retired generals, and five are buried there. It is often called "the town that time forgot." Its population is near 3,800.

The next bridge across the Mississippi is about 35 miles south, at Savanna, Illinois. Hanover, a small town of 1,100, sits on the Apple River, about half of that distance. The town calls itself the "Mallard Capital of the World." Two hundred thousand ducks call Hanover home. They belong to Whistling Wings Inc., a prominent mallard duck hatchery.

Beautiful Mississippi Palisades State Park is located a few miles south of Hanover. Many overlooks on top of the bluff offer spectacular views of the river and the Upper Mississippi Wildlife Refuge. The park is only a short distance from the highway.

Savanna, Illinois, a town of 4,500, dates back to the lead mining era when it was an important shipping port. Indians called it Savanna Manitoumi, meaning "the land of God." It is the hometown of bandleader Wayne King, known as the "Waltz King."

The bridge at Savanna leads to Sabula, Iowa, called "Island City." The island was created by backwater from the building of locks and dams. You reach the small village, population 800, by way of a causeway. Sabula was founded , as a riverport, in 1835. Later it

became involved with commercial fishing, lumbering, and button manufacturing. A rare swing bridge allows four-story towboats to pass through. North America's northernmost grove of hardy pecan trees grow in the rich bottom land of nearby Green Island, Iowa.

To visit Lock and Dam No.12, it will be necessary to go back upriver to Bellevue, Iowa. The city park is an excellent place to watch barge tows slowly slip through the lock.

Bellevue is a town of 2,400 people. Settlers began arriving in 1833. It became an important port and flour milling town. Potter's Flour fed Civil War troops and was shipped nationwide. The huge old mill was built in 1843, making it Iowa's first flour mill.

Mammoth stone warehouses, businesses, and historic old homes, all line the street along the river. All of the buildings face the river, leaving the view unobstructed. Bellevue means, "beautiful view'"

As you travel back downriver, you will notice the backwater which surrounded Sabula, now spreads out, making the next 15 miles of river the widest along Iowa's border. The five-mile width then narrows again at Lock and Dam No.13, at the north edge of Clinton, Iowa.

Clinton, a city of 33,000, was established in the 1880s. It began as a lumbering center and riverport, then grew rapidly with the coming of railroads.

Clinton features a summer Showboat Theatre aboard an authentic paddle wheeler parked on the Mississippi. Riverboat sight-seeing cruises have always been a popular attraction, and are still available today. Full casino gaming and famous prime rib dining were initiated in 1991, on Roberts River Ride paddle wheeler named the Mississippi Belle II.

Riverview Stadium is the home of the Clinton Giants,
the Class A baseball club of the San Francisco
Giants.

Two bridges cross the Mississippi at
Clinton, One goes to Fulton, Illinois, the other to
East Clinton, Illinois.

Fulton was settled by Dutch pioneers in the early
1800s. Agriculture is an important industry in the
area. An authentic Dutch Festival is held each year
in May. Privately-owned Heritage Canyon is located
at Fulton. It is a self-guided nature walk taking you
back to a sample of life in an 1880s settlement,
complete with church and school. This site offers a
beautiful view of Clinton, across the river.

The small community of Cordova, Illinois, is about
25 miles downriver. It as here that the Quad Cities
Nuclear Generating Station looms over the
Mississippi. The station has an information center
which is open to the public.

South of Cordova, Interstate 80 bridges the
Mississippi and enters LeClaire, Iowa. This historic
town, of about 3,000, sits at the head of the upper
rapids, near Lock and Dam No.14. Lock No. 14 was the
last to be improved under the 9-foot channel Act of
1930. It was opened in 1939. The 320-foot lock built
in 1922, now serves as an auxiliary lock.

Le Claire was settled in the late 1830s and named for Antoine Le Claire, an army interpreter, who had purchased a large section of land on the west bank of the Mississippi. The area's first industry was lumbering. The boat-building business thrived a little later, and when Iowa was connected with the eastern United States, Le Claire blossomed into a railroad center.

Buffalo Bill Cody was born near Le Claire in 1846, the same year Iowa became a state. Bill's father built the Cody homestead in 1847. The homestead and Buffalo Bill Museum are open to the public. The museum is an interesting memorial to Indians, pioneers, and old steamboat days.

As the Mississippi leaves Le Claire, it winds through the Quad Cities, all five of them. The cities of Bettendorf and Davenport are on the Iowa side. Moline, East Moline, and Rock Island make up the Illinois riverfront. Originally the term Quad Cities referred to Davenport, Rock Island. Moline, and East Moline. As Bettendorf's population grew and exceeded that of East Moline, the term came to be used for the entire area.

For almost two centuries, the hub of the whole region has been a large government-owned island sitting between Iowa and Illinois. Its importance dates back to 1816 when Colonel William Laurence arrived with orders to establish a fort. The spot chosen was at the southern tip of the island. The name was Fort Armstrong.

During the Civil War, a stockade and wooden shelters housed Confederate prisoners of war. Many died there when a smallpox epidemic took the lives of 500 men.

The government erected the first permanent building in 1864. It was to become the Rock Island Arsenal. The arsenal enlarged for World War I, and continued operating, as one of the largest manufacturing arsenals in the world through World War II.

The island is now called Arsenal Island and is the

headquarters of the Army Weapons Command. Tours of the island are available daily. On display is some of our nation's weaponry, the old Confederate Cemetery, and the home of Colonel George Davenport, one of the early commanders of Fort Armstrong.

The city of Bettendorf, Iowa began in 1840 as the settlement of Gilbert, and was incorporated in 1903. The name was changed to honor an early-day manufacturing family, W. P. Bettendorf and J. W. Bettendorf.

According to Indian lore, Davenport, Iowa is the spot where Marquette and Jolliet chose to camp in 1673. By the 1700s, it was the site of the principal village of the Fox Indians.

The site was part of the large section of land originally purchased by Antoine Le Claire. He eventually sold the area to a group headed by Colonel George Davenport and Russel Farnham. The site was surveyed in 1836, became a town in 1839, and was named for Colonel Davenport. He was a well-known fur trader and operated independently until 1826, when he became an agent for the American Fur Company.

One of the city's very important pioneers was
Daniel D. Palmer who, around 1895, developed the art
of chiropractic medicine. His work was carried on by
his son, B. J. Palmer, and his grandson, David.
The Palmer College of Chiropractic was founded in the

1920s, and still operates today. B. J. Palmer also
pioneered two Iowa radio stations. Station WOC
(wonders of chiropractic) was located at Palmer
College. Sports announcer, Ronald Reagan, was no
doubt its most famous radio personality. Palmer's
other station WHO (with hands only) was located at
Des Moines, Iowa. Even though both stations have
changed owners, the original call letters remain
today.

Davenport was the first Iowa town to be connected
to the eastern United States, when the Rock Island
Railroad built a bridge across the Mississippi River
in 1856. It is the largest of the Quad Cities, with a
population of over one hundred thousand. It houses
one of the world's largest aluminum rolling mills.
Putnam Museum is the third oldest, west of the
Mississippi, and preserves the region's colorful
history. The city hums with activity and projects
connected with Iowa's new gaming industry. The
largest riverboat casino along the state's eastern

coast, is the five-deck President, which docks at the Port of Davenport. It is a beautiful old side-wheeler, 297 feet in length. It boasts 27,000 square feet of gaming space and will accomodate 3,000 guests. It was built around 1930 and was the largest boat on the river, at that time. It is a registered National Historic Landmark.

Moline, Illinois. began in 1848, when a Vermont blacksmith, named John Deere, arrived with his steel plow manufacturing company. Prior to 1837, all plows were made of cast iron. Deere discovered that steel would do a much better job in most soils. He also introduced the first commercially successful riding plow in 1875. It was a horse-drawn rig, called the Gilpin Sulky. Deere's plant provided employment for many and caused Moline to prosper.Most of the city's 45,000 residents are, or have been, somehow associated with the Deere Company activities. Deere's World Headquarters are now located here. Moline is Spanish, meaning "hill."

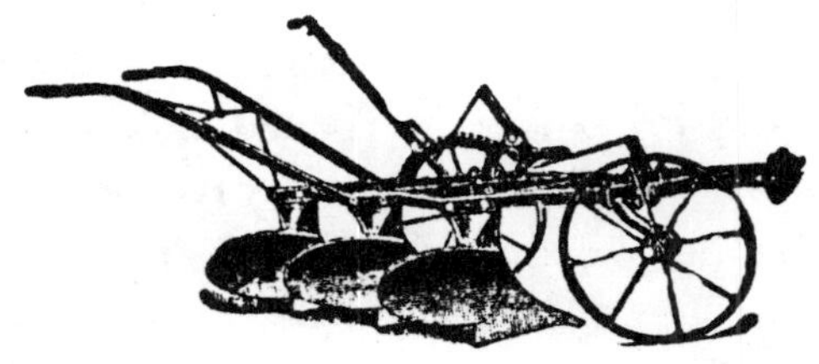

Rock Island, Illinois, is located at the confluence of the Rock and Mississippi rivers. The area was the site of Blackhawk Village, the Sac Indian's principal village.

The earliest white settlement began in 1826, and was called Farnhamsburg, in honor of Russel Farnham. Like Colonel Davenport, Farnham was also in the fur trading business. He was a manager for John Jacob Astor's American Fur Company. The settlement was incorporated in 1837, and the name was changed to Stephenson, in honor of another Army Colonel, at Fort Armstrong. This name lasted until 1841, when it was renamed Rock Island.

The Rock Island Railroad was the first to establish continuous service between Chicago and the Mississippi River.

The years between 1850 and 1890 saw the town as the most active riverport in Illinois. Rock Island was a memorable place for steamboat pilots. The treacherous upper rapids extended nearly 14 miles upriver, to Le Claire. Ragged jutting rocks and swirling currents spanned the width of the river. To add to the natural danger, the Rock Island Line decided to extend its railroad service to the government island , then on to Davenport, Iowa. A railroad bridge was set at the narrowest point on the rapids, and proved to be a greater hazard than the rapids themselves. Only the most experienced steamboat pilots could navigate the long stretch of

rapids and still pass under
the bridge. Shortly after
the bridge was finished, the
Effie Afton went out of
control in the rapids,
struck a bridge pier, and
sunk. She had been loaded
with grain at Cassville,
Wisconsin, and was bound
for St.Louis.A lawsuit

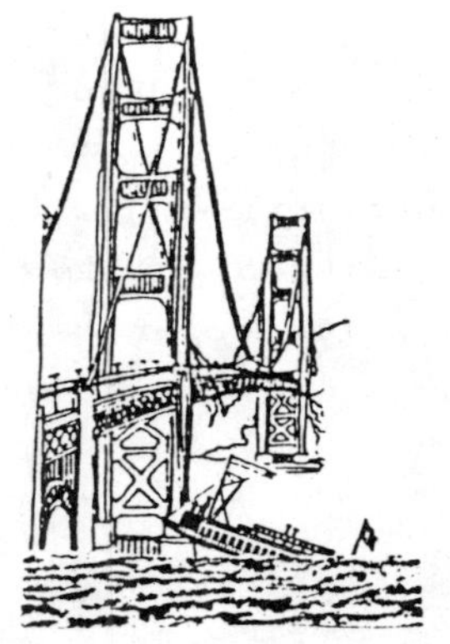

followed which was eventually dismissed, leaving
the railroad blameless. Abraham Lincoln took part in
the case, representing the railroad. In the years
following, many bridges were built, and each one
created a new hazard for steamboats.

The badly located bridge was finally removed.
Since the government owned the island, an important
military installation, the government rebuilt the
bridge. They moved the bridge site downriver to a
safer location. It opened in 1872 and accomodated
both trains and wagons. It is still known as the
Government Bridge. It has been enlarged into a
double-deck structure with a 360° rotating section
to allow towboats to pass through. Trains travel the
upper deck and all other traffic uses the lower
deck.

Rapids piloting was a unique occupation which developed as soon as steamboats began traveling the Upper Mississippi River. Going downriver, steamboat captains would stop at Le Claire and hire a pilot who knew the upper rapids by heart, to guide the boat through to Davenport.

In an attempt to master the upper rapids, a system of buoys was devised in 1879, to guide boats through the twisting channel. Twenty-six buoys were put out each spring. A lamplighter rowed the 17 miles each day to trim and light the lamps on the buoys. They were taken in each fall, before the river froze.

River traffic had to contend with the dangerous rapids well into the next century. Minor improvements were attempted, but progress was slow. Even when ,in 1930, Lock and Dam No.15 was chosen to be the first 9-foot channel structure built, it wasn't until four years later, March 1934, that the upper rapids were finally conquered, seventy-eight years after the Effie Afton went down.

Arsenal Island also houses the Rock Island District of the United States Army Corps of Engineers. Their District Headquarters building, along with a Mississippi River Visitors Center, is located near Fort Armstrong, almost under the Government Bridge. A glass wall of the Visitors Center parallels Lock No. 15 and provides an excellent view of tows "locking through." It is also an extremely interesting view of the rotating section of the Government Bridge above. A movie and several displays pertaining to lock and dam construction and operation are available, and well-informed attendants are on hand, as well.

The Quad-City Metropolitan Area is prosperous and very progressive in all phases of industry and commerce. Its combined population exceeds 240,000. Manufacturing plants are numerous, railroads are busy, and river traffic is heavy. Gaming has proven popular at the Moline-Rock Island docks.

Milan, Illinois, population near 6,300, sits across the Rock River between Rock Island and Andalusia, Illinois. Robert E. Lee's 1837 survey map showed a Town of Milan, which appeared well-established, several miles upriver, at the head of Campbells Island.

Andalusia, Illinois, is a small river town located about eight miles below Milan. Its population may be small, 1,200, but the area contributed greatly to western development. It had one of the most important early-day river crossings above St.Louis. Many of the wagon trains bound for the Oregon Trail, were transported across the Mississippi by Clark's Ferry, at Andalusia.

Highway 92 follows the river to Lock and Dam No.16, then crosses the Mississippi to Muscatine, Iowa.

Muscatine had its beginning when a fur trader was sent to establish a trading post in 1833. Two years later, a woodcutter set up a wood supply business on the riverbank, selling wood to steamboats. At that time, the settlement was simply called Casey's Woodpile. Later it was known as Bloomington, when settlers arrived from Bloomington, Indiana. By 1850, it became necessary to change the name because mail often went to either Indiana or Illinois. In the end, the name Muscatine was chosen, in honor of the friendly Mascouten Indian Tribe. The name is said to mean "place of fire." Mark Twain lived in early Muscatine. He said, "and I can remember Muscatine more pleasantly for its summer sunsets." Quite possibly the Indians were referring to those same sunsets.

Because Muscatine played such a large role in the button manufacturing industry, and because the industry actually started there, it soon became known as "Pearl City." John F. Boepple, a German immigrant, succeeded in making buttons from clam shells, and invented the machinery to do so. Several

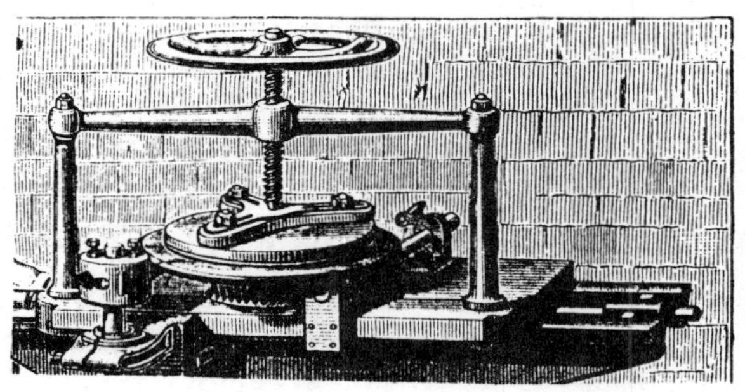

factories located there in the 1890s, with fleets of clammers dredging the Mississippi River.

One of the largest button making operations was the Mc Kee Button Factory. McKee continued making pearl buttons until the mid 1940s, when the cost of clam shells became prohibitive. Plastic was chosen as the material for buttons, but the first buttons made of plastic were not at all serviceable. They melted and disappeared the first time a garment was washed in hot water, or the first time the buttons were touched by a hot iron, whichever came first. This was quickly remedied with adjustments to the mixture. Today a polyester material is used and the McKee Button Factory is still turning out buttons. They also make a machine for sewing buttons on garments.

Clamming is still carried on. Bits of clam shells are now being supplied by Mississippi River fishermen. The pieces are shipped overseas, to be used as seeds for Japanese cultured pearls.

The ever-popular Maid- Rite sandwich originated in Muscatine. In 1926, Fred Angell combined a special cut and grind of beef, and with unique spices, steamed up a delicious non-patty hamburger. Good news travels fast and soon he was receiving requests for his secret recipe. Later that year, franchises were sold to individuals across the country. This

was one of America's first fast-food chains. The four original franchises granted in 1926, are still operating today. An interesting stipulation in those early license agreements, was that the Maid-Rite franchisee "charge at least 10¢" for each sandwich sold. Angell's 1926 Maid-Rite restaurant was ahead of its time, when it provided walk-up windows as a means of convenience. Several generations have eaten Maid-Rites and new franchises are still opening today. If you are lucky enough to find one,and you decide to try the sandwich, one item to remember is that ketchup covers the delicate flavor of the seasoned, choice beef. Mustard, pickles, and onions are the standard dressings.

River cruises are offered at the Port of Muscatine and are an excellent way to view the scenic bluffs that line the river. Muscatine has always been known for its agriculture. Famous Muscatine melons and sweet potatoes are grown in the rich bottomland, on nearby Muscatine Island.

State Highway 22, between Muscatine and Davenport, is a delightful drive. The highway passes near Wildcat Den State Park, and winds through the communities of Fairport and Montpelier, then through the small towns of Buffalo and Blue Grass. Camping

and boating are popular pastimes on this beautiful
section of the Mississippi.

Lock and Dam No.17 sits approximately 20 miles down
the Mississippi, along with Lake Odessa, and the
interesting little community of Toolesboro, Iowa.
Toolesboro is located above the Mississippi, on the
north bank of the Iowa River. The Hopewell Indian
Burial Mounds have been set aside on a 15-acre tract
of land. At this same location, is the historical
marker describing Marquette and Jolliet's visit to
the area, in 1673, when they paddled a short distance
up the Iowa River. The exact spot where they
encountered Indians is unknown. Many consider
Toolesboro to be the location.

The area across the Mississippi, on the west coast
of Illinois, was originally known as Yellowbanks
Territory, because of the color of the sandy soil
along the river. This land was surveyed in 1834, by
Abraham Lincoln. The towns of New Boston and
Keithsburg, Illinois, are directly across the river
from Oakville. There are no bridges here, but in
earlier years, the towns were connected by the New
Boston Ferry. New Boston has a population of 700.
Keithsburg has about 1,000.

The town of Oquawka, Illinois, sits a few miles downriver. Prior to settlement, this area was inhabited by Sac and Fox Indians. Sac is an Indian name, meaning "people of yellow earth." Oquawka began in the 1800s. It experienced a booming river trade and was the last stop on the main stage route between Peoria, Illinois, and the Mississippi

River. The second-oldest Illinois courthouse is still being used at Oquawka. One of the state's few remaining covered bridges.

The community of Kingston, Iowa, is across the Mississippi, just below Oakville. Thomas J. Duryea operated a sawmill in this area in the 1860s, during the lumber industry boom. He processed logs which had been floated down the Iowa and Mississippi rivers. His mill provided building materials and wood for steamboats.

Lock and Dam No.18 sits between Kingston and Burlington. Burlington is one of Iowa's oldest cities, dating back to 1808, when it was a trading post known as Shoquoquon, Indian, meaning "flint hills." The town was platted in 1833 and incorporated in 1836. At that time, a settler from Burlington, Vermont, asked to have the town's name changed to Burlington, and his request was granted. Lumbering was an important industry and during the steamboat era, Burlington was the home port for the Diamond Jo Steamboat Line.

Burlington's first railroad was the C.B.& Q., or (Chicago, Burlington, & Quincy). which opened in 1855. A single-track railroad bridge spanned the Mississippi from 1868 until 1892. That was then replaced by the current double-track bridge.

Burlington was the capital of Wisconsin Territory from 1837 to 1838, and capital of Iowa Territory from 1838 to 1840. One of its early industries was the Mississippi Pearl Button Company. Iowa's oldest newspaper, The Hawkeye, is still being published in Burlington, after moving from Fort Madison in 1839. Burlington Public Library claims to be Iowa's oldest, built from 1896 to 1898.

"Ripley's Believe It Or
Not" called Burlington's
Snake Alley the "crookedest
street in the world" Like
the Fourth Street Elevator
in Dubuque, Heritage Hill
inspired the construction
of Snake Alley, to connect
residents with the downtown.
It was built in 1894. It is
a brick street with five ½
curves and two ¼ curves
descending a distance of
275 feet, or one block, to
the next street below. The
bricks were laid at an
angle to allow better
footing for horse traffic.
Snake Alley is currently
open to one-way traffic.

The Port of Burlington was dedicated in 1928. It
became one of the ports visited by the gaming
riverboat, the Emerald Lady, in 1991. Around 30,000
call Burlington their home town.

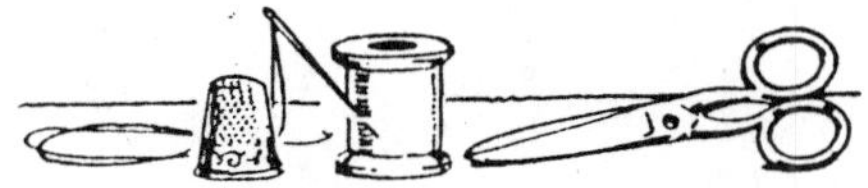

The beautiful flint bluffs to the south of the
city, was another site Zebulon Pike chose in 1805,
for the first fort west of the Mississippi.

The next city down the Mississippi, is Fort Madison, Iowa, with a population of 12,000. Although Pike recommended bluff sites at McGregor and Burlington, the government chose this spot for their fort. It was built in 1808, in conjunction with the Indian factory system. This system was initiated in 1795, and in reality, was a series of warehouses and salesrooms set up to monopolize fur trading with the Indians. This system was abandoned in 1822.

Fort Madison was built on the flat riverbank. The area surrounding the fort was too open to ever be properly protected. In September 1812, Chief Blackhawk, a Sac war chief, not a tribal chief, began attacks on the fort and set fire to the factory. These attacks continued until finally, in 1813, orders were given to abandon Fort Madison. In the dark of the night, troops dug a trench from the fort to the Mississippi. After loading their boats, the soldiers set fire to the fort and crawled back to the river for their escape.

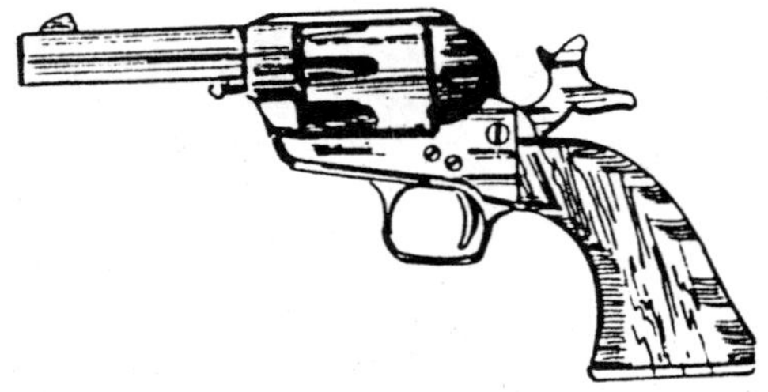

After Indian treaties were signed in 1833, wagon train pioneers and riverboat travelers began settling the area. The town of Fort Madison grew rapidly and Chief Blackhawk became a frequent visitor.

The Lee County courthouse, built in 1843, is Iowa's oldest courthouse in continuous use. The city's cemetery contains the graves of Betsy Ross' daughter, three granddaughters, and one great grandchild. The old Fort Madison has been accurately reproduced by volunteer inmates of nearby Iowa State Penitentiary.

U.S.
MARSHAL

The Atchison, Topeka, and Sante Fe Railroad built a unique railroad bridge across the Mississippi at Fort Madison. It is the longest double-deck. swing-span bridge in the continental United States. Trains travel on the bottom level and autos use the upper deck. The bridge swings open to allow river traffic to pass.

The village of Bentonsport, Iowa, is a few miles west of Fort Madison. It sits on the bank of the Des Moines River, and was an overnight stop for steamboat passengers traveling the Des Moines in the 1880s.

If you cross Fort Madison's swing-span bridge, you will enter what used to be the small community of Niota, Illinois. During the 1993 flood, Mississippi River water savagely scoured the entire area and ruptured a natural gas line.

A few miles downriver is the historic town of Nauvoo, Illinois. Nauvoo has a current population of 1,100, and began as a settlement called Commerce, in 1839.

This was the same year that about 5,000 Mormon refugees were driven from Independence, Missouri. It was the second-largest forced migration in the

history of our country. Led by Joseph Smith, they crossed the Mississippi at Quincy, Illinois, and proceeded upriver to Commerce. Smith changed the settlement's name to Nauvoo, meaning "beautiful place." The town grew rapidly and had reached a population of 12,000 by 1845. It was the largest city in Illinois and the tenth-largest in the nation. Although growth was fast, Nauvoo never knew peace. When Joseph Smith was slain in 1846, the Mormons were forced to flee again. It was then that Brigham Young led the first 400 Mormon families across the frozen Mississippi, and westward to Utah.

A group of French moved to Nauvoo in the 1850s, and left a legacy of wine and blue cheese. These industries flourish today, and the town hosts the annual Grape Festival every Labor Day weekend. Many of Nauvoo's old buildings have been restored and are open to the public.

The bridge at Hamilton leads to Keokuk, Iowa's last riverport. The city was named for Keokuk, a Sac Indian Chief, whose name meant "he who moves around alert." It was originally the site of the Indian village of Puckeshetuk. Later it was known as De Moine Rapids, referring to the rapids above the Des Moines River. Chief Keokuk is buried at Rand Park, overlooking the Mississippi.

Keokuk's first cabin was built in 1820. Many visitors arrived by steamboat in 1828, and a trading post was established in 1829. The first Iowa school on record, was near Keokuk and opened in 1830. Free public schools came in 1829, and free high schools opened in 1911.

Keokuk's heritage is closely tied to the Mississippi River. The first steamboat above St. Louis, arrived in 1819, commanded by Stephen H. Long. This was the end of the line for steamboats until the late 1850s, when a lateral canal was built which by-passed the 11-mile lower rapids.

The city played an important role in the Civil

War. Besides being the swearing-in point for all of Iowa's volunteers, seven army hospitals were built here. War wounded from both sides were transported up the Mississippi on hospital boats. For many it was to be their last trip, The first National Cemetery, west of the Mississippi, was located at Keokuk, and is the only one in Iowa.

Lock and Dam No.19 is at Keokuk. In 1910, the Hamilton Water Power Company began work on a power plant larger than any other, at that time. A dam was built across the Mississippi and a lock was constructed. The operation was then turned over to the Corps of Engineers. The power plant provided electricity for as far away as St.Louis. Today the plant is known as the Union Electric Power Plant and still operates with much of the original equipment. A new 1,200-foot lock was added in 1957, and the original 1913 lock is used as an auxiliary. Summer tours of the dam and power plant are offered daily. The lock is open anytime.

The city operates a museum of river history aboard the old stern-wheel towboat, the George M. Verity. The boat was built in Dubuque, in 1927, and had her first tow from St.Louis to St.Paul, that same year.

About three miles below Keokuk, the Des Moines River forms a small section of the Iowa-Missouri border, then empties into the Mississippi.

The actual boundary between the two states had to be settled by the courts in the 1800s, when a dispute arose over the ownership of an area of bee trees. These trees were quite desireable, as well as valuable, since honey was the only sweetner available to midwest settlers.

Missouri was named for the Missouri Indian Tribe. It is known as the Show Me State and acquired statehood in 1821. Its rich and productive farmland stretches from the corn belt in the north to the cotton belt in the south. The leading crop is soybeans. Other crops include corn, peaches, and

Alexandria, a small Missouri town of about 400, was also completely destroyed by the 1993 flood. Alexandria sat only three miles below the Des Moines River's confluence with the Mississippi. The already-swollen Mississippi refused to accept any more water, and Alexandria was in a direct path of the rampaging Des Moines.

Opposite the mouth of the Des Moines River is the town of Warsaw, Illinois, current population 1,800. During the War of 1812, Warsaw had two military forts. Fort Johnson was built in 1814. Fort Edwards, also a United States fur factory and trading post, was a military installation from 1817 until 1924. The Fort Edwards Monument sits on a high bluff overlooking the Mississippi River. The townsite was laid out in 1834.

The next Illinois river town is Meyer, about 20 river miles below Warsaw. It is the dock site of the Meyer Toll Ferry, which crosses the Mississippi to Canton, Missouri. Ferry service has been an Illinois-Missouri link here since 1843.

Canton sits just below Lock and Dam No.20. It is a scenic river town that incorporated in 1854, and has a current population of near 2,400. Farm implement manufacturing, agriculture, and mining are Canton's most productive activities. The area was severely damaged by a tornado in 1835.

La Grange, Missouri, has a population of 1,200, and is located six miles downriver from Canton. La Grange history goes back to the late 1700s, when it began as a trading post. It is tied to the Civil War by a Union Soldiers Monument, erected in the town square in 1864. It is one of the oldest Missouri towns north of St, Louis. The Mississippi has created a very large island here, called Long Island.

The next bridge across the river is at West Quincy, Missouri, just above Lock and Dam No.21. It connects West Quincy with Quincy, Illinois. During the 1993 flooding, the Mississippi became a river of fire at West Quincy. All barge traffic was suspended in June, and loaded barges were either parked along the river or moved to the Ohio River. A parked barge washed through a break in the levee and rammed a large gasoline station. An explosion followed and burning gasoline quickly spread across the surface of the river.

Quincy was settled in 1822. It was a popular steamboat landing, railroad center, and stove manufacturing city. Quincy Bay is the largest natural harbor on the entire Mississippi. Quincy is located in Adams County. Both were named for John Quincy Adams. To complete the picture, Quincy's town square was John's Square, now Washington Park.

About 15 miles downriver the Mark Twain Memorial Bridge, built in 1935, connects East Hannibal, Illinois with Hannibal, Missouri.

Hannibal was first settled by Moses Bates, on land given as compensation for property damage in the New Madrid earthquake. The town grew when the railroads came in 1856. It now has a population of 19,000. The city basks in the beauty of scenic bluffs and is saturated with reminders of the Mississippi River's most famous steamboat pilot, Samuel Clemens, Mark Twain.

Clemens was born November 30, 1835, about 40 miles southeast of Hannibal, at Florida, Missouri. His sister and other relatives are buried in the Florida Cemetery. By 1863, Clemens was writing under his adopted name, Mark Twain, which he chose because of his love for the river. When navigating the river, steamboat's leadsman would measure the depth of the water. If it were two fathoms (12 feet) deep, he would shout "mark twain", meaning the depth was safe for the boat's passage.

Mark Twain, along with Tom, Huck, Becky, and the rest, still "live" in Hannibal. The Mark Twain Riverboat offers regular river cruises and accomodates 400 passengers. The Mark Twain Cave, a very popular attraction, is just south of the city. The nearby bluffs feature a unique jutting rock formation known as Lover's Leap.

Lock and Dam No.22 sits about nine miles south, at Saverton. Below Saverton, is the scenic river town of Louisiana, Missouri. It was an early-day riverport, and has a current population of 4,500.It began in the eaarly 1800s and is said to have "the most intact Victorian streetscape in the state." Gracious homes are built on high bluffs overlooking the river.

There is no Lock and Dam No.23, but No.24 is located about ten miles south at Clarksville, Missouri. This little village of 600 dates back to 1816. It is noted for its river bluffs and a chain of hills called "knobs." Visitors are offered a skylift ride to the top of the bluff for viewing an Indian Burial Ground, a museum, and the Mississippi River.

Calhoun County, below Pike, Illinois, is a narrow strip of land sandwiched between the Mississippi and Illinois Rivers. The towns of Hamburg, Hardin, and Batchtown nestle in beautiful rolling hills. Parks and waterfowl reserves dot the land along both rivers. Indians knew this area as "the gathering of the waters." Near Brussels, a free ferry crosses the Illinois River and docks at the town of Grafton, where the Illinois joins the Mississippi.

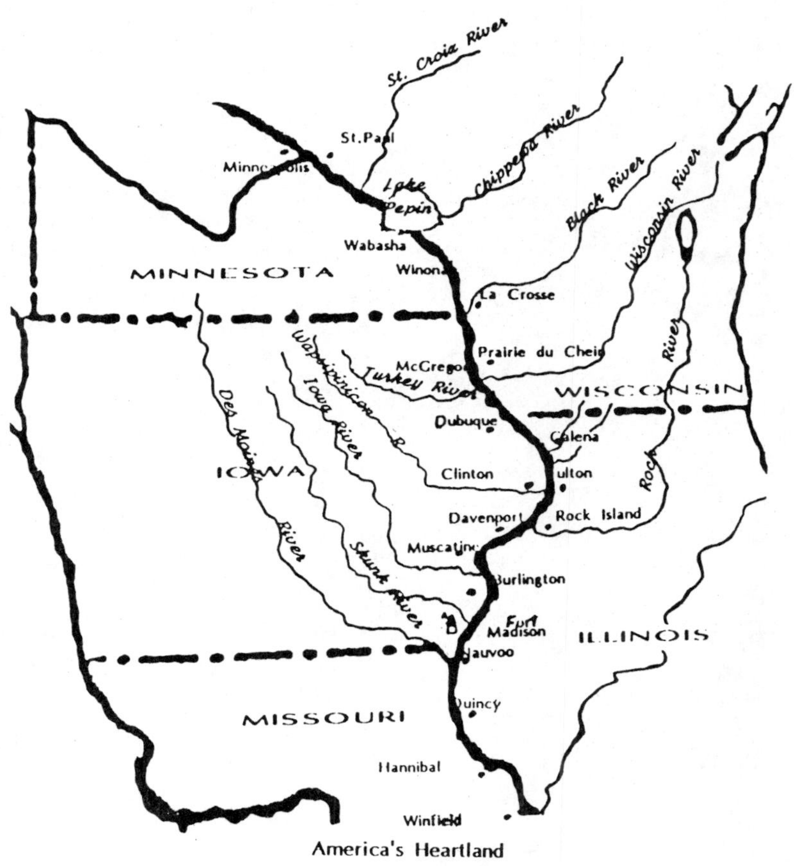

America's Heartland

Chapter Four

CROSSROADS OF AMERICA

When Marquette and Jolliet visited the Illinois and Mississippi confluence in 1673, they recommended using the Illinois River as a connection between Lake Michigan and the Mississippi. It wasn't until 1848, almost two centuries later, that the Illinois-Michigan Canal opened. By 1933 the canal was improved and enlarged. The 327-mile barge route is now 60 feet wide, 9 feet deep and has seven locks and dams capable of lifting vessels 10 feet to 40 feet. Dams at Peoria and La Grange are both moveable,

and are raised during periods of low water. Cargoes
are exchanged at La Salle, Illinois. The importance
of this waterway was surpassed only by the Erie
Canal.

Grafton, Illinois was founded in 1830, and was a
very important riverport during the steamboat era.
Today it has a population just over 1,000. Many of the
shops and homes are of native limestone. Nearby Pere
Marquette State Park, Illinois' largest, encompasses
8,000 acres and overlooks both rivers.
The area's limestone bluffs are very similar to the
White Cliffs of Dover.

The town of Elsah, Illinois is about six miles
below Grafton. It is a 19th Century village sitting
between high forested bluffs and the Mississippi.
Its streets and bridges are extremely narrow and
buses are discouraged. Elsah's population is near
1,000.

Alton was founded, as a steamboat landing, in 1816.
Nearby outcroppings of coal and limestone made the
area quite desirable, and the town grew rapidly. It
was named for a son of Colonel Rufus Easton, a

St.Louis lawyer , who laid out the townsite. Alton
was a very busy riverport by the 1830s, and an early-
day rival of St. Louis. The state's first
penitentiary was constructed there in 1833.

Robert Pershing Wadlow, the world's tallest man,
was born, at Alton, in 1918. Although no abnormal
rate of growth was noticed early, his growth began to
accelerate when he was eight, and finally he reached
eight feet eleven inches in height. Alton calls him
their "gentle giant." He passed away in 1940, at the
áge of 22.

Although the economic growth Alton hoped for
happened across the Mississippi, Alton did continue

to grow and prosper. Today, along with East Alton, it
is busily occupied by refineries, flour mills,
manufacturing, and still has a large volume of river
traffic. Riverboat gambling occupies boats in
Alton's Marina. Factories fill the river plain in the
lower town, while the residential area sits on the
bluff above.

Alton is located at the northern end of the
American Bottoms, an area of rich alluvial deposits,

plenty of water, and an excellent agricultural climate. The area gained that name in the late 1700s, to distinguish it from the Spanish-owned land west of the Mississippi. Most of the fruit, vegetables, and grain found in early trading posts, was from there. The American Bottoms extend south, about 100 miles, to Chester, Illinois.

Lock and Dam No.26, at Alton, was built in 1938. As river traffic increased on both the Mississippi and Illinois rivers, the lock soon became the largest bottleneck on the river. As a remedy, Congress authorized a larger structure to be built below Alton. A new 1,200 foot lock opened in 1989, and a 600 foot auxiliary lock is to be available in 1993. the old dam was dynamited and removed from the river. The old lock sits idle, near the Alton Marina.
Alton's Clark Bridge, a narrow span leading to Missouri, is also being replaced by a new wider bridge.
keelboat, which had to be sent back to St. Louis when the river became too narrow, at what is now North Dakota. The rest of the party continued on in two dugouts and six canoes.

The Mississippi, which has been fairly clear in color, now becomes the brown color of the Missouri. When Marquette saw the muddy Missouri gushing into the Mississippi, he wrote, "I have seen nothing more frightful." Farmers describe the Missouri as "too thick to drink, and too thin to plow." Big Muddy is the Mississippi's longest tributary.

Between Alton and Granite City, Illinois, the Mississippi flows around and between islands. At two locations, ledges of rock extend under the river from the east bank, causing a sharp increase in the slope of the river. This obstacle is known as the Chain of Rocks Reach.

There are 669 miles of river between the first lock at St. Anthony Falls, and the last at Granite City. A total of 29 structures handle a river fall of about 400 feet. Except for power facilities at Minneapolis, Minnesota, Rock Island, Illinois, and Keokuk, Iowa, all dams were built for navigational purposes. All locks operate 24 hours a day, and there is no charge for any boat to lock through.

East St.Louis, Illinois is the next downriver town. It was platted in 1859, and by 1918, was a leader in animal feed products, aluminum, and railroad repair work. Today it is an important industrial city of 55,000 people.

A few miles south is Cahokia, the oldest community in Illinois. It was founded in 1699 as a French-Canadian Mission, and named for the Cahokia Indians. The name means "wild geese." It became the county seat for the state's first French county, St. Clair County, which formed in 1790. The oldest courthouse west of the Allegheny Mountains, was erected here. Cahokia also had the first Illinois school. Today the city lists a population nearing 19,000. The county seat was moved to Belleville in 1814.

Belleville is French, meaning "beautiful village." The first circulation library opened there in 1836. Illinois' first railroad operated between Belleville and the Mississippi River. Belleville's population today is over 42,000.

Nearby Cahokia Mounds Historic Site displays a prehistoric Indian City. Monks Mound, the largest, surpasses the size of the Pyramids of Egypt.

Dupo, Illinois, is seven miles downriver from Cahokia. Interstate 255 West will lead to the Jefferson Barracks Bridge, and the St. Louis area.

St. Louis began in 1764. Through a trading rights grant, the Louisiana Fur Company set up a trading post 17 miles below the junction of the Missouri and Mississippi rivers. For its first 53 years of existance, the town was a collection point for furs from the north and west.

Growth was slow until the early 1800s. On August 2, 1817, the city's first steamboat, the Zebulon M. Pike, docked at the port. Two years later the Independence sailed up the Missouri River to Franklin, in central Missouri.

95

This created a new gateway to the west and St. Louis bloomed. By the mid 1800s, it had advanced to the nation's leading inland city, and third busiest port.

One of St. Louis' earliest industries was steamboat building. In 1890, the Wainwright Building became the city's first skyscraper.

A stage between Kaskaskia, Illinois, and St. Louis made its first regular run in 1819. 

Steamboat travel and the city of St. Louis suffered a major set-back one May evening in 1849, when a fire broke out on the White Cloud, one of the many steamboats anchored at the landing. Boats near the White Cloud began to catch sparks and burn also. Some of the burning vessels were cut loose to drift downriver. As they slowly made their way out to

96

the main current, they would bump into still other
boats, and immediately another fire would break out.
The fires lasted well into the next morning, and when
the last spark died, 23 steamboats and the entire
business district had been destroyed.

Ferry service across the Mississippi came early to
St. Louis. Service between Illinois and Missouri
began in 1797. In 1819, Samuel Wiggins received a
franchise that gave him a monopoly, and by the time
the railroads reached the Mississippi, he controlled
all river traffic. It was about this time that some
St. Louis folks felt the need for a bridge across the
Mississippi. Captain James B. Eads, of the Corps of
Engineers, was called upon to design the bridge and
direct its construction. Being quite experienced in
the use of steel, he chose to build a very ornate
triple-arch steel bridge. It was financed by the sale

of bonds, completed in 1874, and was operated as a
rental, or toll, bridge. The Wiggins Ferry Company
retaliated with fierce competition of rates. Only a
few would pay the price to use the bridge, and bonds
were soon in default. The Eads Bridge did manage to
survive, and today the beautiful structure is being
preserved by the City of St. Louis.

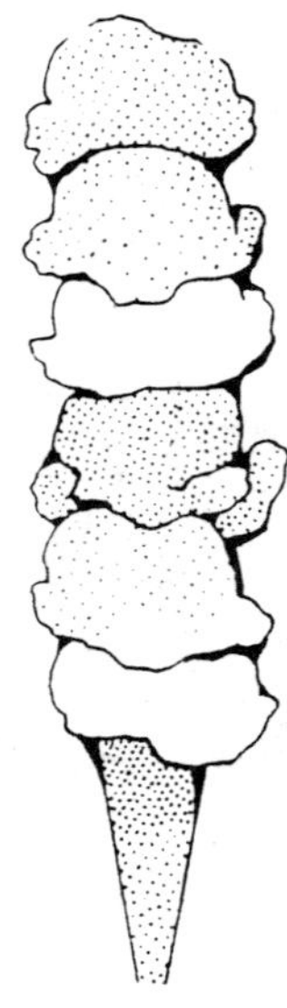

St. Louis hosted the 1904 Louisiana Purchase
Expedition World's Fair. A brand new item, the ice-
cream cone was introduced at that time.

Gateway Arch towers 630 feet above the riverport.
It is taller than the Washington Monument and over
twice the height of the Statue of Liberty.
Construction was completed in 1964 and trips to an
observation room at the top of the arch are
available. Windows on both sides of the room provide
a breath-taking 30-mile panoramic view.

The trip begins 50 feet below ground by entering a unique capsule transporter, called a tram. Each tram is made up of eight barrel-shaped capsules, joined together like a train. These operate on special tracks up the legs of the arch. Each capsule holds five people and has a leveling device to keep passengers in a normal position. It takes less than five minutes to reach the top and the view is spectacular.

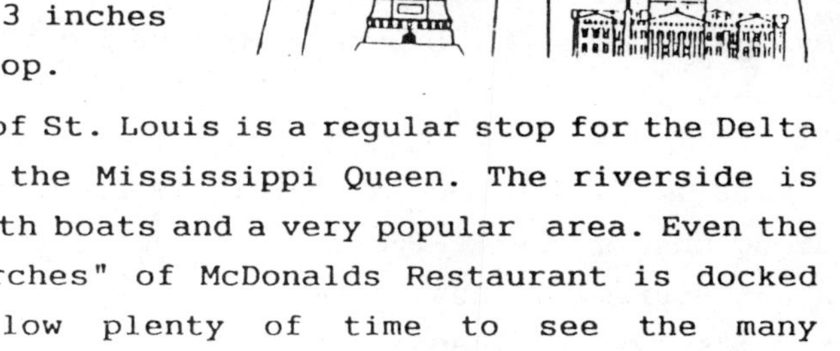

The arch is located on top of St. Louis' 52-foot-high flood wall. This 11-mile barrier was severely tested during the 1993 flood, when the Mississippi crested to within 3 inches from the top.

The Port of St. Louis is a regular stop for the Delta Queen and the Mississippi Queen. The riverside is crowded with boats and a very popular area. Even the "golden arches" of McDonalds Restaurant is docked there. Allow plenty of time to see the many attractions in the St. Louis area. It is a major

transportation hub, a port of entry, and the center
of the Great Lakes to Gulf Waterway....an important
part of the "Crossroads of America."

This area of the Missouri River is very interesting
as well as rich in history. Portage Des Sioux is a
Missouri community, of around 500
people. It is situated on land
between the Missouri River and
the Mississippi. Spaniards erected a fort here, in
1799, to protect a portage between the rivers. The
two-mile portage saved a river trip of 25 miles.

West Alton, Missouri, population 34,000, also sits
between the two rivers. The Clark Bridge crosses the
Mississippi, and leads to Alton, Illinois. The Lewis
Bridge crosses the Missouri, and handles traffic to
St. Louis.

Fort Belle Fontaine was built, in 1805, on a bluff
along the Missouri River,
about four miles above the
Mississippi confluence. The site
of the fort and factory proved
to be very unhandy and a new site
was chose some 300 miles to the
north, above the mouth of the
Des Moines River. This would be Fort Madison, Iowa,
and also proved to be a bad choice.

St. Charles, Missouri, sits on tall bluffs
overlooking the Missouri, about 21 miles above the
confluence. The town began in 1769, making it one

of Missouri's earliest towns. It became the state's first capital in 1821. It was first known as Les Petites Otes, meaning "The Little Hills." The city is a commercial shipping center for farm produce, and has a population of over 37,000. A toll ferry across the Missouri operates here.

As you leave St. Louis, again going downriver, the Missouri cities of Oakville, Arnold, Imperial, Kimmswick, Sulphur Springs, Barnhart, Pevely, and Herculaneum are all very old and very industrial. It is difficult to tell where one ends and the next one begins. They all seem to be industrial extensions of St. Louis.

Below Herculaneum, the Mississippi winds through tree-lined bluffs, and through the twin cities of Festus and Crystal City, then on to Ste.Genevieve, another 29 miles downriver.

Old Ste.Genevieve records go back to 1715 with the discovery of nearby lead ore. Settlements began around 1730 on flat swampy ground along the Mississippi. In 1785 the river flooded and destroyed the village site. Residents were forced to higher ground, about two miles back from the river. This is the town's present site. It became an important riverport for shipping lead, salt, and grain. The current population is 4,500, and still growing.

The Ste. Genevieve-Modoc Ferry docks here and crosses the Mississippi to Illinois, where the road leads to Prairie du Rocher, population 700. This is one of Illinois' oldest towns. It was founded in 1772, by the French. During the 1993 flood, when it seemed impossible to keep the angry Mississippi from washing Prairie deu Rocher off the face of the earth, city officials made a bold decision. Against the advice of the Corp of Engineers, they decided to intentionally break the levee to open a gigantic drainage hole, which would divert flood waters away from town. Their efforts saved Prairie du Rocher. Downriver is Fort Kaskaskia Historical Site, the Kaskaskia River Lock and Dam, and the Kaskaskia's confluence with the Mississippi.

Back on the west bank of the river, is St. Marys, Missouri, a town deserted by a river. A bridge at the east edge of town has a sign reading "Mississippi River" and does span a small stream of Mississippi backwater. This was the main river channel until the 1799 flood. It was then that the Mississippi changed its course, and moved over to the Kaskaskia River channel, about six miles to the east. The road across this bridge is the only access to Kaskaskia Island, which was the townsite of Kaskaskia, Illinois' first state capital. Kaskaskia is an Indian tribal name, meaning "uncertain." The town was founded in 1703. The site became an island in 1799, and was completely destroyed by the 1881 flood. This is the location of the "Liberty Bell of the West," which is 11 years older than the bell at Philadelphia. When the 1993 flood again washed over askaskia Island, the 252-year-old bell was used to warn anyone still on the island.

The first bridge across the Mississippi, since leaving St. Louis, is near St. Marys and leads to Chester, Illinois, called "River City." Chester lies at the southern point of the American Bottoms. The town is also the "Home of Popeye the Sailor," and proudly displays a bronze statue of him in Segar Park. Menard Penitentiary is built in the bluffs, and nearby Mary's River Covered Bridge is a popular attraction. The Pierre Menard Home State Historic Site, called "Mount Vernon of the West," offers many special events. Menard was Illinois' first Governor.

Illinois 3 highway continues downriver to the small town of Grand Tower, population 750. Rock formations here are excellent for hiking and exploring. Devil's Backbone State Park is at the north end of town. Suspension Pipeline Bridge, the Texas-Illinois natural gas pipeline, was built on the rock formation in 1954. It measures over 600 feet in length, making it one of the world's longest.

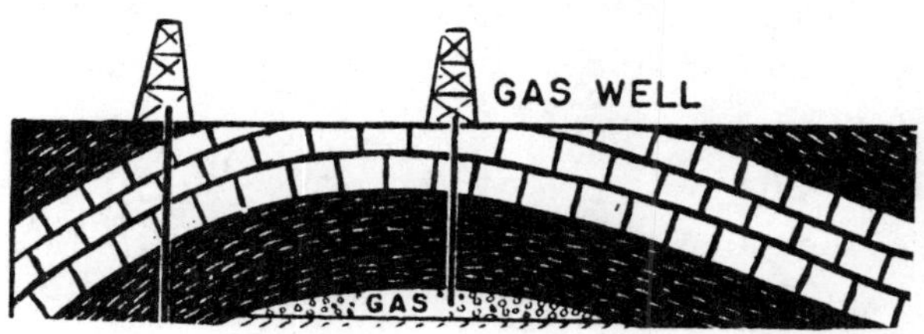

Grand Tower offers an excellent view of Tower Rock, a rock formation 85 feet in height, protruding out of the Mississippi.

The Illinois towns of Wolf Lake, Ware, and Jonesboro lie south of Grand Tower. This is Illinois' western section of the Trail of Tears route.

Early maps named the site Cape Girardot. Most of its history began with a trading post around 1705. Permanent settlement started in 1793 and gave the city its present name spelling. It is an industrial city and a major shipping center. Industries include meat packing, cement, clothing and shoes.

At one time Missouri had 30 covered bridges. Today only four remain, and three of those are near the Mississippi River. The oldest and longest of these three is the Burfordville Covered Bridge, a few miles west of Cape Girardeau Building on it began in 1858, but was delayed because of the Civil War, and was not finished until 1868. It is 140 feet long, 12 feet wide, 14 feet high, and spans the Whitewater River.

The Bollinger Mill (grist mill) is at this same location. The mill site dates back to 1800 Spanish land grants to George Bollinger, in return for developing 640 acres and bringing more eastern settlers to the area. Today's structure is the third to be built on the site. Union soldiers partially burned the mill during the Civil War. The mill can still operate today.

North of Cape Girardeau is the beautiful Trail of Tears State Park, which contains a small portion of the route of the 1838 forced migration, where they crossed the Mississippi River.

As eastern states became more populated, residents asked the government to evict the Indian population. Congress passed the Indian Removal Act in 1830, allowing the President to move eastern tribes to more sparsley settled land west of the Mississippi River. Within 10 years the government moved over 70,000 Indians of the Five Civilized Tribes: Choctaw, Cherokee, Chickasaw, Creek, and Seminole. The section of route near Cape Girardeau, was traveled in late 1838, and early 1839. Fifteen thousand southern Indians were herded, in snow and cold, across Georgia, southern Illinois,across the

Mississippi, and on to
Oklahoma. It is estimated
that as many as 5,000
Indians died because of
this ordeal. To add insult
to injury, each Indian
was forced to pay sixteen
cents per day for the
trip. This amount was then
deducted from the price
they were forced to sell
their land for.

Back across the river and south, is the town of
Thebes, Illinois. This was once a
bustling riverport. The courthouse
was built in 1845. Abraham Lincoln
once practiced law here.

Horseshoe Lake, between Thebes and Cairo, calls
itself the Goose Capital of the World. Numerous
hunting clubs dot the area.

Several bends later, the Mississippi arrives at
Cairo, Illinois, which is situated in a three-state
corner. Illinois, Missouri, and Kentucky meet
here.

Cairo is the county seat of Alexander County, Illinois first. Settlement of Cairo was attempted in 1818, but only the name survived. The second attempt was in 1837. Growth was slow, but the town hung on until the railroad arrived in 1855. When the Illinois Central opened a track between Chicago and Cairo, the city immediately became an important cotton port.

This area of southern Illinois is often called "Little Egypt," because of its resemblance to the east bank of the Nile. Cairo was named by a St.Louis merchant who also saw the similarity. The city is saturated with history. It was made a Port of

Delivery in 1854. The Custom House was started in 1867, and completed in 1872. The first floor was the post office, government offices occupied the second, and the third was the United States Courtroom. The city's public library opened in 1884, and is almost like a museum today.

Cairo was often flooded in the early days, before river control was initiated. Today the city is completely surrounded by levees and floodwalls built on top of levees. Heavy rains deluged the Mississippi Valley in 1937. At Cairo, the water level rose 56 feet.

Cairo is where the Beautiful Ohio meets the Mighty Mississippi, but neither river seems to be impressed by the other. The clear blue Ohio water refuses to merge with the brown Mississippi. Fort Defiance State Park sits between the two rivers, and overlooks this strange meeting. A sign there labels it "the Confluence of America." The Ohio carries twice as much water as the Mississippi, and is its largest tributary. As it travels toward its mouth, the Mississippi gets narrower and deeper. Here it is one mile wide and 87 feet deep. At its mouth it is one-half mile wide and 129 feet deep.

Cairo is a very busy industrial port on the Beautiful Ohio. It is a large shipping center for cotton, grain, and fruit. The city has two bridges. One crosses the Mississippi to Charleston, Missouri, population 5,000. The other spans the Ohio River to Wickliffe, Kentucky. The Mississippi now leaves Illinois after being its boundary from top to bottom. Illinois is 400 miles long and unofficially known as "the tall state." Its name is the French equivalant of Iliniwek, which were area Indians whose name meant "men."

As the Mississippi leaves Cairo, its course becomes a series of broad loops, horeshoe bends, and cut-offs. Flooding can cause it to change its channel completely.

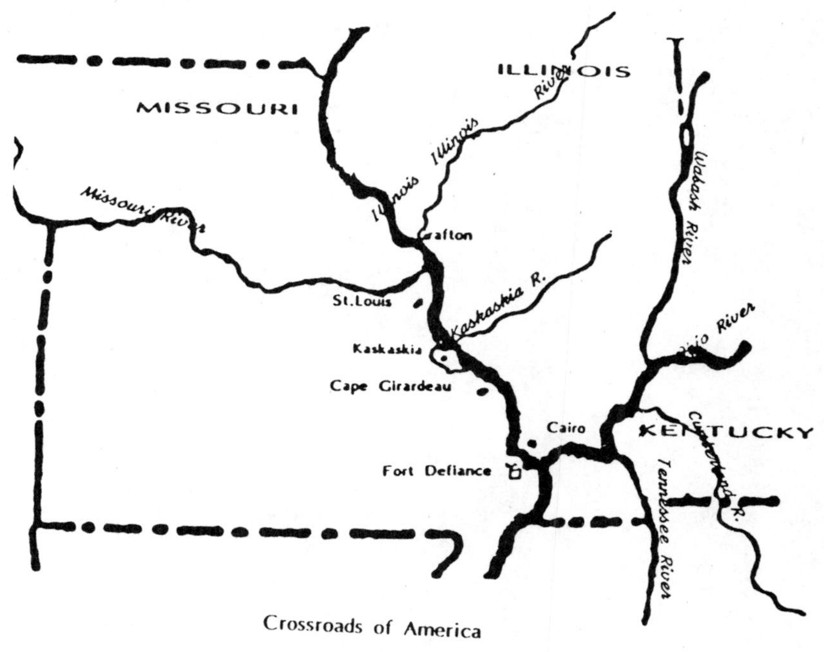

Crossroads of America

Chapter Five

THE OLD SOUTH

Cairo is the gateway to the Lower Mississippi River Valley. This is where the "Old South" begins, and the Mississippi becomes "Old Man River." It is a region of plantations, swamps, and bayous. Cypress, palmetto, live oak, and Magnolia trees thrive in the most fertile river bottomland in our nation.

American colonists had been familiar with the cotton plant since 1621 and Eli Whitney's cotton gin had been around since 1793. Conditions were excellent here for growing cotton as a crop. The area

was sparsely settled, land was cheap, and river transportation was available. The mid-1800s were cotton's prosperous times. Other crops including tobacco, rice, and corn thrived also.

The Mississippi has always been a strong willful river. Before levees, its natural flow way, or channel, was some 40 miles wide.

There are six river basins in the Lower Valley: Upper Mississippi, Ohio, Missouri, Tennessee, Red, Cumberland, White, and Arkansas. Wet years would turn the Mississippi into a raging sea.

The first levees were built by the French, on the east bank, near New Orleans in 1717. Then came levees on the west bank, restricting the river's width to less than 10 miles. By the 1830s, compulsory levee building laws were enacted. The higher the levees, the worse the floods. The river was too over-powering. It became impossible for the settlers to comply with levee laws, it was too expensive. They felt they needed federal assistance and persistently asked for it. In 1879, Congress created the Mississippi River Commission, and informed them their duties were to protect river banks, improve river channels, and prevent destructive flooding.

The first government appropriation was made in 1881 under the Rivers and Harbors Act, and appropriations continue today.

The next 47 years saw a constant battle between the Mississippi flooding, and Congress passing new flood control acts to provide additional funding. The 1927 flood caused a major levee failure just north of Greenville, Mississippi, and drove 600,000 from their homes. Finally, in 1928, new programs were implemented. From Cape Girardeau, Missouri, to below New Orleans, the Corps of Engineers built 1,600 miles of levees, measuring from 15 feet to 40 feet in height, longer than China's Great Wall.
Levee heights were raised along the Upper Mississippi in 1952 after what was then called a 100-year flood, and strengthened after the even-worse flood in 1965. With the record-breaking flood in 1993, new political issues have arisen where levees are concerned, which may take years to resolve. Issues are of no interest to the river. It continues to flood if it wants to. It continues to shorten its trip to the Gulf by cutting across broad loops and horseshoe bends. Its will is only bent, not broken.

It is said LaSalles 1,300 mile float trip, 300 years ago, is probably mostly solid ground today. Who knows what the next 300 years will bring?

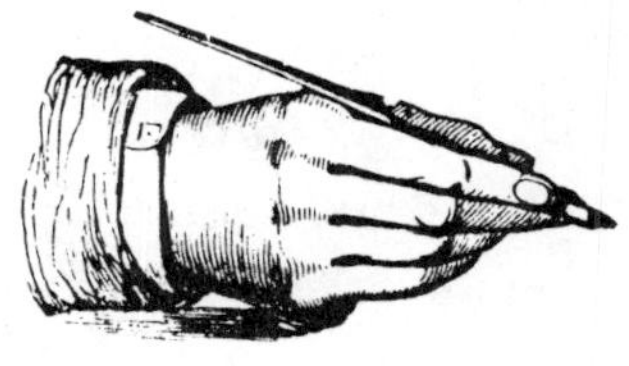

Columbus, Kentucky, is another 20 miles south of Wickliffe. Belmont Battlefield State Park features the massive chain and anchor used by Confederate

forces to block Union gunboats, during the Civil War. A huge chain was stretched across the river on rafts. This fortified position was known as "The Gibralter of the West." A toll ferry operates here.

Kentucky's last river town is Hickman, population just under 3,000. There is no bridge across the Mississippi, but ferry service is available. From here, the two river channels loop northward around Sassafrass Ridge, then back south toward Tennessee.

The Mississippi River Bridge, at Cairo, leads to Charleston, Missouri, an attractive town of over 5,000. The town has many beautiful old mansions.

About 35 miles down the Mississippi is the colorful old river town of New Madrid, Missouri, home to about 3,200 people. The town originated as a trading post in 1783, and has been forced to relocate several times, due to floods and earthquakes. Earthquakes on the night of December 11, 1811, and again on January 7, 1812, shook the area violently. The earth literally opened up and changed the course of the Mississippi River channel. Mew Madrid was also the site of a fierce Civil War battle.

Many towns have either been left high and dry by
river channel changes, or inundated by flood waters.
New Madrid has several structures that are on
rollers, in case a move is necessary.

The Hunter-Dawson Historic Site, the old home of
William Hunter, is surrounded by some of Missouri's
oldest trees. Hunter was a local merchant and owner
of a sawmill in the late 1850s.

The lowlands south of New Madrid are ideal for
growing cotton, soybeans, and peaches. Missouri's
last two river cities are Hayti, and Caruthersville,
with populations of 4,000 and 8,000 respectively.
Caruthersville was settled in the late 1700s by a fur
trader. The 1811 earthquake destroyed the original
site.

The Mississippi Bridge outside of Caruthersville,
is Missouri's last, and leads to Tennessee.

Tennessee, the Volunteer State, joined the Union
in 1796. It is named for the Cherokee Indian village
of Tanasi. It is a wide state stretching from the
Great Smoky Mountains to the Mississippi River. Its

roots grow deep. It was first explored by Hernando de Soto in 1541, when he discovered the Mississippi River.

For emergency food for his party of 700, de Soto brought the first swine into our country. Since that time, "de Soto Original Pork Barbeque" has developed into a southern favorite.

Tennessee has emerged from its historic past, and with little effort, entered the atomic age. It is the center for country music. The Grand Ole Opry was first broadcasted , from Nashville in 1925, as the "Barn Dance," and is still aired today. The state's crops include tobacco, cotton, and soybeans.

Tiptonville, Tennessee, north of Caruthersville, sits on Reelfoot Lake. This is the mid-south's largest natural lake. It was created by the 1811 New Madrid earthquake, when it was left by the Mississippi River's change of course. It is eerie and swamplike.

The river angles away from most roads in Tennessee, and the next city of any size will be Memphis, about 100 miles to the south.

Back on the west bank of the Mississippi, the river leaves Missouri about 15 miles below Caruthersville, and becomes Arkansas' eastern boundary.

Arkansas is an Indian name, meaning "downstream people." It gained statehood in 1836, and since that time, has had many names. It has been known as the Bear State, and the Bowie State. In 1953 the state adopted Land of Opportunity, and lately it has been called The Natural State,and Bill Clinton's State. From the Ozarks to the Delta, Arkansas is blessed with many great rivers and lakes. It is where you

"ease on down the road." Its peaceful life was shattered by the Civil War. Many fierce battles were waged there, between 1862 and 1864, resulting in thousands of deaths. The state blends the deep South with the pioneer West.

As with most states along the Mississippi River, lumbering was a prime industry in early history. Today its products include cotton, poultry, rice, and soybeans.

River traffic became insignificant in the 1880s, because of silt deposits and the arrival of railroads. However, river improvements have renewed shipping interest. The Arkansas River Project, which includes 11 dams and reservoirs has made the lower one-third of the Arkansas navigable.

Osceola, Arkansas was originally called Plum Point. It was founded in 1830, by William B. Edrington. He bartered a site from the Indians to establish a refueling station for steamboats, more commonly called a wood yard. The town was named for the famous Seminole Indian leader. Today, food processing, and light industry support the economy. Fruit of the Loom and American Greeting Cards are among the industries.

The nation's largest privately-owned farm is at Wilson, Arkansas. The 47-square-mile-plantation is owned by Lee Wilson & Company, for whom the town is named. Wilson's population is 1,100. The Hampson Museum State Park offers displays of artifacts taken from the nearby Indian mounds.

Memphis was a United States fort in 1797. Settlement began in 1819. It sprawls on the Chickasaw Bluffs, above the Mississippi, where Arkansas, Tennessee, and Mississippi meet. It was named for the ancient Egyptian city.

In early days it was a Chickasaw Indian village.

Memphis was a military center early in the Civil War. It was the site of one of the most decisive battles, and one of the shortest. In 1862, while spectators watched, the city was captured by a Union gunboat force in a battle that only lasted 20 minutes. It remained occupied until the end of the war.

The 1870s' Yellow Fever epidemic devastated Memphis, killing 8,000 residents. The city was ruined until drastic sanitary reforms were initiated. By 1900, it had regained its position as the state's leading city.

Memphis is a major cotton market, and has sponsored a cotton carnival each May, since 1931. One legend maintains this is where de Soto first saw the Mississippi.

Memphis has a large port area on Presidents Island, which is created by the main river channel on one side, and a second channel, called Harbor Channel,

The Loosahatchie and Wolf rivers, along with many other creeks, flow into the Mississippi here. Flooding has been a problem at Memphis.

Memphis is where civil-rights leader, Dr. Martin Luther King was slain in 1968. He was felled by a sniper's bullet as he stood on the balcony of the Lorraine Motel. The room he occupied has now been developed into a National Civil Rights Museum.

The city is very modern, and in keeping with the Egyptian theme, a beautiful 32-story sports complex was completed in 1991. It is called The Great American Pyramid. The unique structure really adds to the beauty of the downtown district.

America's only Mississippi River Museum & Park is at nearby Mud Island. Construction began on this interesting display in 1977 and it opened in 1983. The indoor museum is arranged in eight general catagories: First River People, History and development of river transportation, the Packet Boat, Towboat, River Legends & Disasters, Civil War, River Music and a 4,000 gallon aquarium,called the River Room.

The outside Riverwalk features a flowing scale model of the lower Mississippi, with 1,200,000 gallons of water running through the system. The Gulf of Mexico is a special surprise.

Memphis is just another word for music, especially "blues." The historic five-block district around Beale Street, is a mecca for musicians, and all music-lovers in general. This is where the blues was born. The Memphis Blues, the first blues song published, was written here.

Certainly, one of Memphis' most popular tourist attractions is Graceland, home of Elvis. Several different package tours are available: The Mansion Tour, The Elvis Presley Automobile Museum, The Lisa Marie and Hound Dog II Jet Planes, the Sincerely Elvis display of momentos, the Walk A Mile in My Shoes, or Platinum Tour,which is all of the above.

Both bridges at Memphis cross the Mississippi into Arkansas. To the south are the Arkansas towns of West Helena and Helena, with a combined population of 21,000. Helena sits closer to the Mississippi and the city has a paved levee road that leads to a nice new riverside park. There are many historic structures preserved in both towns.

About 35 miles to the west, is the Louisiana Purchase Marker State Park, which is the "0" point for land surveys of the Louisiana Purchase. The park includes 36 acres within a headwater swamp. A boardwalk provides access to the monument in the swamp.

Another interesting place is the White River National Wildlife Refuge, near St. Charles, Arkansas. It covers 100,000 acres of wetlands and Mississippi River backwaters. Below that is the Arkansas Post National Monument and Arkansas County Museum. Both commemorate the first European settlement in the lower Mississippi River Valley, established in 1686, by Henri De Tonti. They also commemorate the birth of the state of Arkansas.

Because its eastern part was a vast swamp, it barely had the minumum 50,000 residents required for statehood.

In May 1861, Arkansas seceded from the Union and Arkansas went to war. By mid-1862, Union gunboats controlled most of the Mississippi River and were threatening Vicksburg. When gunboats approached the White River into Arkansas, the Confederates began preparing to defend the Arkansas River, which was a direct water route to Little Rock. By the end of the year, an earth fortification was completed, and called Fort Hindman, or Post of Arkansas. On January 5, 1863, a 30,000-man army and the entire Mississippi fleet prepared to attack Fort Hindman. The Confederates, while anticipating an attack,

never imagined the numbers would be so large. When
the Confederate Commander asked for instructions, he
was ordered "to hold out until help arrives or until
all are dead." The attack began January 10, and was
over by the next afternoon. They did not hold out
until all were dead, the Union took about 4,800
prisoners. Most of Fort Hindman was destroyed. What
was left is now deep in the Arkansas River.

Dumas, Arkansas, a town of 6,100 is about 20 miles
south of the Arkansas Post, then McGehee, population
just under 5,700. The next river community is
Arkansas City, 700, located below the confluence of
the White and Arkansas rivers with the Mississippi.
This was an important riverport until the river
changed its channel in the devastating 1927 flood.
There are several streets which go to the road on top
of the levee.

Lake Village, Arkansas is a city of 3,100, where an
interesting tourist information center perches on
stilts in Lake Chicot. The lake was once a bend of the
Mississippi, but about a mile from the channel
now.

Eudora, population 3,800 is Arkansas' last river
city. It is 17 miles downriver.

Arkansas' last bridge across the Mississippi leads to Greenville, Mississippi.

Mississippi is the Magnolia State, with statehood dating back to 1817. It was the home of Choctaw, Chickasaw, and Natchez Indian Nations. With the arrival of European settlers, and a series of treaties, Indians were moved to the Oklahoma area. Mississippi's way of life is rural and unhurried. Time doesn't stand still in Mississippi, but it runs slower. Cotton, soybeans, rice, and oats are the state's important crops. The 1927 Mississippi River flood left 100,000 Mississippians homeless, and in 1973, another flood drove 50,000 from the Delta area.

There is only one Mississippi River crossing between Memphis, Tennessee, and Greenville, Mississippi. That is the bridge at Helena, Arkansas.

Friars Point, Mississippi is about 14 miles south of Helena. It was incorporated in 1853, and was first called Farrar's Point.

Rosedale, Mississippi is an additional 40 miles from Friars Point. This is a little larger town with a population of 2,800. It is the site of the Great River Road State Park, and the welcome center steamboat replica, The River Road Queen. The park is located inside the batture, the area of land between the levee and the river. The batture here is three miles wide. Arkansas' White River meets the Mississippi, just above Rosedale, and the Arkansas flows in immediately below the town. Some think this is where Hernando de Soto first saw the Mississippi, where he died, and where he was buried.

Greenville is the next downriver city. It has a current population of 40,000, and is an important commerce center. It is Mississippi's largest riverport and the river can even handle low-draft ocean vessels.It has several industrial sites. It is

a major riverboat building center, and is home to the largest builder of flatbottom boats in the world. Vlasic Pickles processes 96 varieties here. The city has the largest rice processing plant in the nation, and the largest rice exporting facility in the Southeast. Greenville is one of Mississippi's three regular stops for the Delta Queen and the Mississippi Queen.

After the 1927 flood, higher levees were built around Greenville.

The Leroy Percy State Park ,
a few miles south of Greenville,
offers visitors a chance to
view the alligator population.
A raised boardwalk spans their
hot artesian water home.

Long stretches of flat Yazoo Delta farmland occupy
the area from Greenville to Vicksburg, Mississippi.
The average width of the delta is 65 miles. It is
extremely fertile. Bumper crops of rice, cotton and
soybeans grow here. The flatland gives way as you
near the city of Vicksburg. Just north of the city, a
navigation channel connects the Yazoo and the
Mississippi rivers. Experimental Station farms are
growing cotton of different colors. Red, brown,
green, and blue have been tried so far. The
Mississippi changed its course in 1876. It left most
of Vicksburg to the Yazoo River, which now occupies
the old Mississippi channel. Vicksburg's population
is near 25,000. The city has always been an important
riverport, and seems blanketed in history and
tradition.

The first French settlement was built high on the bluffs in 1718, but it was wiped out by Indians in 1729. The town incorporated in 1825, and was named for Reverend Newitt Vick, a minister. The Civil War left Vicksburg with the burden of heavy losses of life. The Vicksburg National Military Park marks the positions of both the Confederate and Union troops in its 1,741-acre area. It is a very impressive place to visit, but allow plenty of time to cover the grounds.

The bridge crossing the Mississippi, leads to Louisiana, the Pelican State. It also calls itself the Bayou State. It dates back to the early 1700s when Pierre Iberville located the mouth of the Mississippi River. The great population migration began in the early 1800s, bringing Louisiana statehood in 1812.

It is the only state bisected by the Mississippi and it has long had to contend with the unruly forces of the river. The 1927 flood was devastating and in 1937, when heavy rains caused the river to go out of its banks, New Orleans was saved only by dynamiting the city's levees. This allowed the water to spread out.

From the confluence of the Red River to the Gulf of Mexico, any flooding causes the Mississippi River's course to be lost in a maze of cross channels, called bayous. A bayou is defined as a creek, or minor river that is a tributary of another body of water. The Chocktaw Indian name for creek was "bayuk." The French translation, of course, was bayou.

Fur trapping has been important to Louisiana since the days of the first settlers. Today the state is the leader in sales of muskrat, mink, otter, raccoon, and nutria pelts. Agricultural crops include cotton, rice, soybeans, sugarcane, sweet potatoes, corn, wheat, and strawberries.

The highway out of Vicksburg leads to Tallulah, Louisiana, a nice city of 10,400, then north to Lake Providence Louisiana. about 6,400. This town sits on a large lake of the same name, which is a bend of the Mississippi left high and dry, when the river changed its course. It is a port city. Cotton, rice and other agricultural products leave on barges for New Orleans. The Terral Barge line operates here and the Hollybrook Seed Company distributes cotton seed

Back on the Mississippi side at Vicksburg, along highway U.S. 61, south of town, the roadsides are a profusion of green vines covering everything that stands still. This plant is Kudzu, once thought to be the answer to erosion. When its growth could not be controlled, it became more of a problem than the problem. It now is very common all over the South.

A scale model of the lower 500 miles of the Mississippi River is on display at the Waterways Experiment Station. It is used for river control studies.

Twenty-eight miles south of Vicksburg, Port Gibson, Mississippi, sits on a curve of the Little Pierre. It is a 200-year-old port, originally called Gibson's Landing. It was founded in 1788 by Samuel Gibson, a plantation owner.

The Civil War had a heavy impact on Port Gibson. General Grant declared it "too beautiful to destroy," and spared it was.

One of the town's nearby attractions is the Ruins of Windsor, the remains of a very large and very old mansion, built in 1861. Windsor survived the Civil War, only to be burned to the ground by a careless smoker, in 1890. It was used as an observation post by Confederates, and after the Battle of Port Gibson, as a  Union Hospital. It was the landmark for Mississippi River steamboat pilots. The old town of Bruinsburg, Mississippi, sat below Windsor on the Bayou Pierre, almost at its confluence with the Mississippi. The road between Port Gibson and Bruinsburg is the route General Grant used to get to Vicksburg. A ferry operates in this area and connects Mississippi to St. Joseph, a small Louisiana town of about 1,700 people.

Port Gibson's First Presbyterian Church is famous
for the gold hand atop
the steeple, ever pointing
toward heaven. The first hand
was made of wood, but had to
be replaced in 1901. From
the sidewalk to the tip of
the finger measures 147 feet.
The hand is ten feet, four
inches in length: the index
finger is four feet in length.
The chandeliers in the church
came from the Robert E. Lee steamboat.

Tours of the nearby Grand Gulf Nuclear Power
Station are available. Grand Gulf is one of the most
modern generating facilities of electricity in the
world. The 500-foot cooling tower is the tallest
concrete structure in the state.

Rosalie Abraham
operates the
Visitors Center
in Port Gibson.
She has a stand
of brown cotton
at her home. She
spreads southern
hospitality, is
helpful and gives
"Mississippi Hugs.

The Natchez Trace winds 450 miles, from Natchez, Mississippi to Nashville, Tennessee, through deep dark forests, lush green vegetation, and beside clear  trickling streams.This scenic route is over 8,000 years old. It was originally " traced out"by buffalo, then followed by Indians, and finally trampled into a crude road by traders, trappers, and missionaries. The early Postal Service used the Trace to deliver mail, and Andrew Jackson led his troops on the path on their way to the "Battle of New Orleans," in 1815. Flatboats floated their cargoes downriver to New Orleans markets, but their return trip north was along the Trace. From 1800 to 1820, it was the busiest highway in the Southwest.About 20 inns (called stands) were built along the Trace.Most provided only the bare necesities. Mount Locust, near Natchez, was built in the late 1700s, and has been restored.

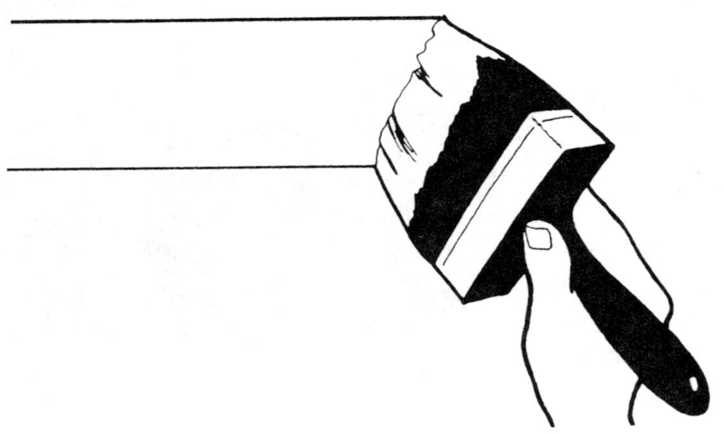

The community of Lorman, Mississippi, is nine miles south of Port Gibson, just off the Trace. Be sure to visit the Old Country Store, near the "Crossroads of History," the junction of the Natchez Trace and the old El Camino Real.The store was established in 1875, making it one of Mississippi's oldest businesses.The building was constructed in 1890, and most of the fixtures date back to that same time. Ceilings are 14 feet high, rolling ladders travel the length of the store for shelves too high to reach,a cheese cutter used daily for the past 70 years, and an 11-foot high shoe case with a wind-up motor, are all part of the wonders of the store. Other features are a free museum, plenty of souvenirs, and some of the best hand-packed ice cream you've ever tasted.

The most scenic and most direct route to Natchez, Mississippi, is the Trace. Natchez is the oldest city in Mississippi and the oldest riverport. It began with land grants to French settlers in 1702. Actual settlement started, on the bluffs in 1716, as Fort Rosalie, incorporated in 1803, and chose its name to honor the Natchez Indian Tribe. It grew up around a trading post and  became an important shipping point for cotton.

The entertainment district, Natchez-Under-the-Hill, was once known as
the "Barbary Coast of
the Mississippi." The
city is famous for its
beautiful antebellum
mansions of the 1800s,
large plantations, and
colorful gardens.

Current population of Natchez is 22,000. The state
passed a law, in 1990, allowing river gaming, which
was initiated in 1992.

Although Woodville, Mississippi, is not on the
Mississippi River, it must be included since it is
only 35 miles south of Natchez. This small town is
practically a complete historic district in itself.
Rosemont Plantation is the boyhood home of Jefferson
Davis.

To get back to the Mississippi River it is
necessary to go back to Natchez and cross the bridge
to Vidalia, Louisiana.

The little town of Waterproof, Louisiana is
located about 22 miles north of Vidalia. In very
early days, the El Camino Real passed through and
crossed the river to get to Mississippi. The
Plantation Pecan Company operates in Waterproof.

Vidalia is a small town of 6,000. It is surrounded
by agriculture. Light industry and shipping make up
the economy.

To continue downriver from Vidalia, Louisiana 15,
which follows the Mississippi, is a well-traveled
highway. Most of the road is either built on top of
the levee, or cut out along the side of the levee.
Once in awhile it is possible to get a glimpse of the
river, but the batture is wide here, and planted in
crops. The highway passes through Deer Park, the
Three Rivers Wildlife Area, and arrives at the Corps
of Engineers' Old River Project.

OLD RIVER PROJECT

Old River was once a loop of the Mississippi. It has
flowed in both directions in the past, today it
doesn't flow at all. It was a 7-mile-cutoff, left
behind when the Mississippi changed its course,160
years ago.

When the first settlers arrived, they found the Red
River emptying into a bend of the Mississippi, and
the Atchafalaya River serving as a well-defined
distributary. In 1831 Captain Henry Shreve cut

across the neck of the Mississippi river bend, below
the Red River confluence. The Mississippi readily
accepted the shortcut and abandoned its old
channel.

The Red no longer flowed into the Mississippi, but into the Atchafalaya. The Old River merely connected them to the Mississippi. Its current usually flowed west, from the Mississippi toward the Atchafalaya, however during high water periods on the Red River, the flow sometimes reversed.

The headwaters of the Atchafalaya had been blocked for years by a massive 30-mile-long log jam. In 1839 the State of Louisiana began removing the logs to open up the river. As a result, the Atchafalaya became deeper and wider, and carried more and more of the Mississippi's flow. It offered the Mississippi a shorter outlet to the Gulf of Mexico, 142 miles compared to 315 miles. It became apparent that unless something were done, the Mississippi would change course by capturing the Atchafalaya. The effects would be devastating for all of the areas along both rivers.

In 1954 Congress authorized the Old River Control Project. Construction began the next year on structures, inflow and outflow channels between the Red and Mississippi rivers, a navigation lock, and an earthen dam, which closes the Old River. The lock is 1,185 feet long and 75 feet wide. Highway 15 crosses over the lock on a lift-span highway bridge. The project was completed in 1963, and of course is operated by the Corps of Engineers.

Floods in 1973. 1974, 1975, and 1979 damaged the control structures. Repairs and modifications were made, but left areas of concern. In 1985 an auxiliary structure, with a new inflow channel, was built and operates along with the original one.

Simmesport, Louisiana, with a population of near 2,300, sits on the Atchafalaya, which carries a controlled one-fourth to one-third of the combined Mississippi-Red rivers' water to the Gulf. It is flowing away from the rivers and therefore is classified as a distributary rather than a tributary. The Atchafalaya, which is Chocktaw, meaning "long river," is about 170 miles in length and is the major distributary for the rivers. It enters the Gulf of Mexico, below Morgan City, Louisiana.

Morganza, Louisiana, has a population of under 1,000. It sits on a large loop , or bend, of the Mississippi. Below that is New Roads, 3,900, not directly on the river, but on a large lake abandoned by it. A ferry operates across the Mississippi to St. Francisville, Louisiana. This is also a small town established in 1785, on a ridge above the river.

Baton Rouge, Louisiana, began as a fort in 1719. It grew as a riverport,and incorporated in
1819. Its name means "red stick."
It was named by the French for
a red cypress post that marked
a boundary between Indian
tribes.

The city sprawls along the east bank of the Mississippi, about 80 miles northwest of New Orleans. Its port, Port Allen, is at the head of deepwater navigation.

Baton Rouge is Louisiana's capital, and the business of the state is carried on at the 34-story Capitol Building, built in 1932. Besides the state offices, this building has an ornate Memorial Hall, and an observation tower. The city's population is over 219,000. The bridge across the Mississippi leads to Port Allen, population 6,000.

Older highways between Baton Rouge and New Orleans dip and dodge around and along canals and bayous. Newer ones bridge a lot of the swampy area. The Bonnet Carre Spillway, built in 1932, is below Baton Rouge. This is another diversion of Mississippi floodwater. It connects the river with Lake Pontchartrain. When flooding threatens, water can be forced through the spillway and the lake into Mississippi Sound, east of New Orleans. The Morganza Floodway is still another diversion.

Lake Pontchartrain is very large. The causeway across the lake to New Orleans is the world's longest bridge, 28 miles, over water.

New Orleans, city of 557,000 plus, "The City that Care Forgot." Chocktaw, Chickasaw, and Natchez Indians were its first inhabitants. In 1718, hundreds of French colonists arrived in Louisiana and settled at the present site of the city. The heart of the city is the famous French Quarter, the very oldest part of town. Jackson Square is flanked by many historic buildings. Some streets still bear the names given them in 1718.

Serious fires ravaged New Orleans in 1788 and again in 1794. The city has seen its share of war. Jean Lafitte, notorious pirate leader, joined American forces in the War of 1812. He aided in the British defeat at the Battle of New Orleans, in January of 1815.

New Orleans has always been a good-time town. It staged the first Mardi Gras parade in 1838. The name applies to only one day, the day before Ash Wednesday, and means "Fat Tuesday," but now includes the entire festival period. In 1857, the street pageants began to assume their present format, and the first night parade was held.

By 1840, the city was the world's fourth ranking port. Steamboats left port traveling upriver at about six miles per hour. Boats returning from the north breezed into port at about twelve miles per hour.

In 1970, the city began a 30-year project, called Centroport USA, to switch much of the port's busy activities from the Mississippi to wharves and industrial complexes along the Gulf. The intention is to free the river frontage for more residential and recreational use. The Mississippi-Gulf outlet, part of a system of channels between the river and Gulf, has shortened ship passage by 40 miles. Freighters and tankers from all over the world assemble here.

Two bridges cross the Mississippi River. The Huey
P. Long Bridge accomodates U.S.90 and the Public Belt
Railroad. Including approaches, it is over four
miles in length. The Greater New Orleans Bridge
handles the downtown traffic. It is over two miles
long. Its main span rises 150 feet above the river. In
addition, the Jackson Avenue Ferry and the Canal
Street Ferry both carry traffic across the river.

The city is divided by the Mississippi River
flowing from the west to the Gulf. The terrain lies
about five feet below sea level. The first levee on
the Mississippi, was built here and was three feet
high. An interesting note today, is the amazing
difference between the street level and the top of
the levee. During periods of high water, the river
surface may be 10 to 20 feet above the street. The
city has over 100 miles of levees and a drainage pump
system that can draw billions of gallons of water a
day.

The Mississippi can be viewed at the Rivergate
Exhibition, the Moon Walk River Observation, and the
observation deck on top of the Trade Mart Building.
All are located in the downtown area.

The New Orleans Mint, which operated from 1838 to
1861, and 1879 to 1909, is now under the jurisdiction
of the Louisiana State Museum. At its peak it could

produce $ 5 million in coins each month. The huge
Louisiana Superdome towers over downtown New Orleans
and the Mississippi. It opened in 1975 and seats over
95,000. New Orleans is the last city on the river, and
a fitting climax to the Old South.

The Old South

Chapter Six

THE DEEP DELTA

After the Mississippi River leaves New Orleans, it continues south another 100 miles before reaching the Gulf. Louisiana 23 , known as the Belle Chasse Highway, follows the river through about a dozen communities to Venice,Louisiana, the dot at the end of the Great River Road.

Belle Chasse is the largest of the towns with a population of 5,400. A ferry connects the town with the east bank of the river.The road then passes

through several small
communities, all engaged
in farming, cattle raising,
or citrus growing. Oranges
grown here are extra sweet.
The Orange Festival is
held in conjunction with
the Plaquemines Parish
Fair, each December.

West Pointe a la Hache has a very busy ferry. It is
large and able to accomodate most types of vehicles.
It goes to Pointe a la Hache, on the east bank of the
Mississippi.

Port Sulphur, about 3,400, is primarily involved
in the sulphur industry. Buras is the next town of any
size. Almost 4,200 live here. Shipping is heavy all
along this section of the Mississippi. The last
Natural Historic Landmark on the river is old Fort
Jackson. six miles below Buras.

Prior to October 1795, Spain kept the mouth of the
Mississippi River closed to all except Spanish
vessels, and a few privileged ships. The Treaty of

San Lorenzo opened the river to all navigation, and was the first step in the emergence of New Orleans as a world port.

Construction on Fort Jackson began in 1822. It was built in a star-shaped pentagon. The walls were 25 feet above the waterline of the moat which completely surrounded it. They were 20 feet thick. In the center of the fort was a bomb-proof shelter, accomodating 500 men. By 1832, it was finished and occupied by a small force. Twenty years later, threat of the Mexican War prompted the President to officially declare it a military reservation. Occupation of the fort was an on-again off-again matter depending on wars. It was used as late as World War I, as a training base, then sold to a private individual in 1927.

It sat idle for the next 33 years, reverting to a snake-infested jungle. In 1961 it was declared a National Historic Monument and restoration began. It sits 32 nautical miles from the Gulf of Mexico, 22 miles from the lighthouse at the head of passes, and 65 miles southeast of New Orleans.

Between Fort Jackson and
the Mississippi is the La
Salle Monument, which
commemorates the discovery
of the mouth of the
Mississippi River, now
the state of Louisiana,
in 1682, by French
explorer Rene-Robert
Cavelier de La Salle.
It is located atop
the levee bordering
the river. It was
erected by Plaquemines
Parish Commission
Council and dedicated
in 1967.

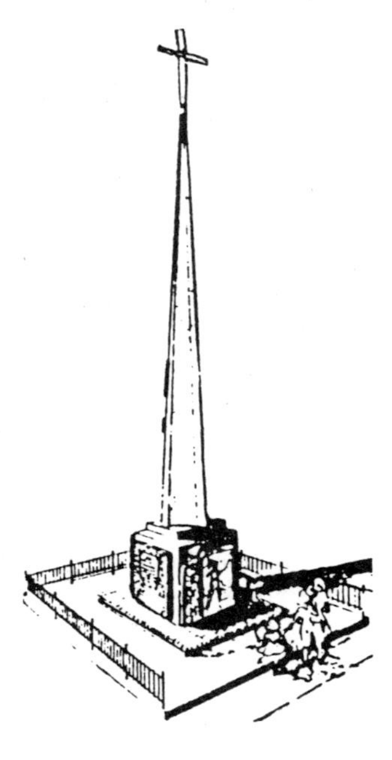

Venice, Louisiana, the
last town on the map, is
a very small community,
but is bustling with
various activities and it
seems to be growing in
in size. It is home port
for a very large fleet
of fishing boats. Some
large, and some small,
some new, some old.

Venice is also the hub of Louisiana's offshore oil industry. One of the largest fields in the world is located in the Gulf of Mexico. The lower harbor in Venice is filled with major oil company vessels and drilling outfits.

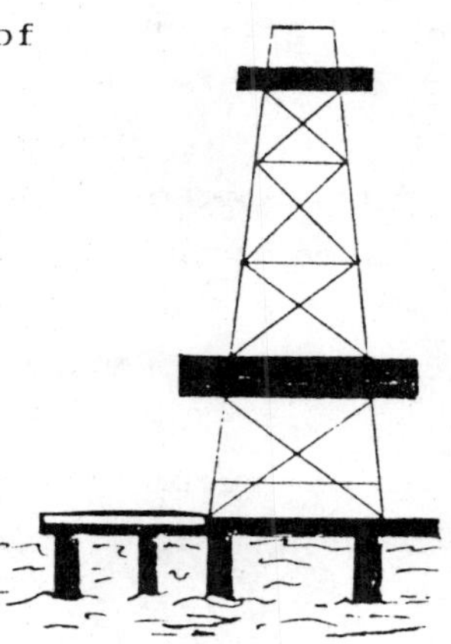

Hurricanes have taken their toll around Venice. The town is ever-changing, trading old buildings damaged or blown away by storms, for new ones. Everyone seems to keep their same location, only the buildings change.

Immediately below Venice, the Mississippi channel begins to branch off and divides into five separate channels, called "passes," which empty into the Gulf.

Early French navigators favored Southeast Pass and built an outpost, called Balize, to protect New Orleans. The first Civil War river battle was fought at the Head of Passes in 1861. This was one of the few Confederate naval victories of the war. Some dry years saw little water and vessels could not find an

open channel between the river and the Gulf. In 1875 Congress contracted with river engineer, James B Eads, to open a reliable channel. He had just completed the St. Louis Bridge the year before. Eads built a system of jetties on the South Pass and within four years, the river had dug itself a 30-foot-deep route to the sea. In the early 1900s a similar jetty system created a 40-foot channel in the Southwest Pass. This has become the major route for oceangoing vessels today.

Pilottown, Louisiana, two miles in from Head of Passes, is the interchange point where bar pilots and river pilots replace sea pilots on ocean vessels. Bar pilots meet the ships at sea and guide them through the Passes, up to Pilottown. River pilots take over there for the journey to ports on the Mississippi. The process is reversed on outgoing trips.

There is a lighthouse at the Head of Passes, and a partial ghost town on Southwest Pass, called Burrwood. The only way to reach any of the delta below Venice, is by boat. Delta is defined as nearly a flat plain through which the diverging branches of a river run, as it nears its end. A delta is not carved

by the river, it is built by the river. The areas
deposited between the passes are called subdeltas.
About four hundred million tons of mud are left in the
subdeltas each year. The delta is growing into the
Gulf of Mexico at the rate of about one mile every 16
years.

Humidity causes the clouds over the delta to swirl
like water in the gentle Gulf winds. Its hard to tell
whether they are welcoming the Mississippi to the
sea, or if they are warning it of unseen dangers.
There is beauty here, but its melancholic, as we say
goodbye to the Mighty Mississippi.

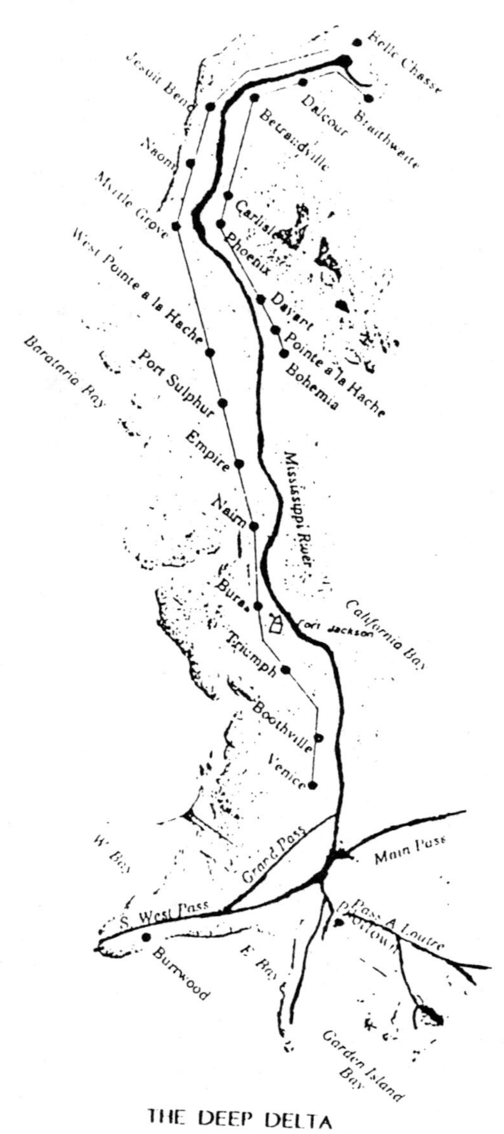

THE DEEP DELTA

MISSISSIPPI RIVER BASIN

Need a Gift?

For

- **Shower** • **Birthday** • **Mother's Day** •
- **Anniversary** • **Christmas** •

Turn Page For Order Form
(Order Now While Supply Lasts!)

TO ORDER COPIES OF

ON THE SHOULDERS OF A GIANT

Please send me _____ copies of On the Shoulders of a Giant at $9.95 each.

(Make checks payable to QUIXOTE PRESS.)

Name _______________________________

Street _______________________________

City _____________ State _____ Zip Code _____

SEND ORDERS TO:

QUIXOTE PRESS
31798 K18S
Sioux City, IA 51109

TO ORDER COPIES OF

ON THE SHOULDERS OF A GIANT

Please send me _____ copies of On the Shoulders of a Giant at $9.95 each.

(Make checks payable to QUIXOTE PRESS.)

Name _______________________________

Street _______________________________

City _____________ State _____ Zip Code _____

SEND ORDERS TO:

QUIXOTE PRESS
31798 K18S
Sioux City, IA 51109

INDEX

H

I

Since you have enjoyed this book, perhaps you would be interested in some of these others from QUIXOTE PRESS.

ARKANSAS BOOKS

HOW TO TALK ARKANSAS
    by Bruce Carlson .... paperback $7.95
ARKANSAS' ROADKILL COOKBOOK
    by Bruce Carlson .... paperback $7.95
REVENGE OF ROADKILL
    by Bruce Carlson .... paperback $7.95
GHOSTS OF THE OZARKS
    by Bruce Carlson .... paperback $9.95
A FIELD GUIDE TO SMALL ARKANSAS FEMALES
    by Bruce Carlson .... paperback $9.95
LET'S US GO DOWN TO THE RIVER 'N...
    by various authors .... paperback $9.95
ARKANSAS' VANISHING OUTHOUSE
    by Bruce Carlson .... paperback $9.95
TALL TALES OF THE MISSISSIPPI RIVER
    by Dan Titus .... paperback $9.95
LOST & BURIED TREASURE OF THE MISSISSIPPI RIVER
    by Netha Bell & Gary Scholl .... paperback $9.95
TALES OF HACKETT'S CREEK
    by Dan Titus .... paperback $9.95
UNSOLVED MYSTERIES OF THE MISSISSIPPI RIVER
    by Netha Bell .... paperback $9.95
101 WAYS TO USE A DEAD RIVER FLY
    by Bruce Carlson .... paperback $7.95
VACANT LOT, SCHOOL YARD & BACK ALLEY GAMES
    by various authors .... paperback $9.95
HOW TO TALK MIDWESTERN
    by Robert Thomas .... paperback $7.95
ARKANSAS COOKIN'
    by Bruce Carlson .... (3x5) paperback $5.95

DAKOTA BOOKS

HOW TO TALK DAKOTA .... paperback $7.95
Some Pretty Tame, but Kinda Funny Stories About Early
DAKOTA LADIES-OF-THE-EVENING
    by Bruce Carlson .... paperback $9.95

SOUTH DAKOTA ROADKILL COOKBOOK
        by Bruce Carlson .... paperback $7.95
REVENGE OF ROADKILL
        by Bruce Carlson .... paperback $7.95
101 WAYS TO USE A DEAD RIVER FLY
        by Bruce Carlson .... paperback $7.95
LET'S US GO DOWN TO THE RIVER 'N...
        by various authors .... paperback $9.95
LOST & BURIED TREASURE OF THE MISSOURI RIVER
        by Netha Bell .... paperback $9.95
MAKIN' DO IN SOUTH DAKOTA
        by various authors .... paperback $9.95
GUNSHOOTIN', WHISKEY DRINKIN', GIRL CHASIN' STORIES
OUT OF THE OLD DAKOTAS
        by Netha Bell .... paperback $9.95
THE DAKOTAS' VANISHING OUTHOUSE
        by Bruce Carlson .... paperback $9.95
VACANT LOT, SCHOOL YARD & BACK ALLEY GAMES
        by various authors .... paperback $9.95
HOW TO TALK MIDWESTERN
        by Robert Thomas .... paperback $7.95
DAKOTA COOKIN'
        by Bruce Carlson .... (3x5) paperback $5.95

ILLINOIS BOOKS

ILLINOIS COOKIN'
        by Bruce Carlson .... (3x5) paperback $5.95
THE VANISHING OUTHOUSE OF ILLINOIS
        by Bruce Carlson .... paperback $9.95
A FIELD GUIDE TO ILLINOIS' CRITTERS
        by Bruce Carlson .... paperback $7.95
YOU KNOW YOU'RE IN ILLINOIS WHEN...
        by Bruce Carlson .... paperback $7.95
Some Pretty Tame, but Kinda Funny Stories About Early
ILLINOIS LADIES-OF-THE-EVENING
        by Bruce Carlson .... paperback $9.95
ILLINOIS' ROADKILL COOKBOOK
        by Bruce Carlson .... paperback $7.95
101 WAYS TO USE A DEAD RIVER FLY
        by Bruce Carlson .... paperback $7.95

HOW TO TALK ILLINOIS
        by Netha Bell .... paperback $7.95
TALL TALES OF THE MISSISSIPPI RIVER
        by Dan Titus .... paperback $9.95
TALES OF HACKETT'S CREEK
        by Dan Titus .... paperback $9.95
UNSOLVED MYSTERIES OF THE MISSISSIPPI
        by Netha Bell .... paperback $9.95
LOST & BURIED TREASURE OF THE MISSISSIPPI RIVER
        by Netha Bell & Gary Scholl .... paperback $9.95
STRANGE FOLKS ALONG THE MISSISSIPPI
        by Pat Wallace .... paperback $9.95
LET'S US GO DOWN TO THE RIVER 'N...
        by various authors .... paperback $9.95
MISSISSIPPI RIVER PO' FOLK
        by Pat Wallace .... paperback $9.95
GHOSTS OF THE MISSISSIPPI RIVER (from Keokuk to St. Louis)
        by Bruce Carlson .... paperback $9.95
GHOSTS OF THE MISSISSIPPI RIVER (from Dubuque to Keokuk)
        by Bruce Carlson .... paperback $9.95
MAKIN' DO IN ILLINOIS
        by various authors .... paperback $9.95
MY VERY FIRST
        by various authors .... paperback $9.95
VACANT LOT, SCHOOL YARD & BACK ALLEY GAMES
        by various authors .... paperback $9.95
HOW TO TALK MIDWESTERN
        by Robert Thomas .... paperback $7.95

INDIANA BOOKS

HOW TO TALK INDIANA .... paperback $7.95
INDIANA'S ROADKILL COOKBOOK
        by Bruce Carlson .... paperback $7.95
REVENGE OF ROADKILL
        by Bruce Carlson .... paperback $7.95
A FIELD GUIDE TO SMALL INDIANA FEMALES
        by Bruce Carlson .... paperback $9.95
GHOSTS OF THE OHIO RIVER (from Cincinnati to Louisville)
        by Bruce Carlson .... paperback $9.95
LET'S US GO DOWN TO THE RIVER 'N...
        by various authors .... paperback $9.95

101 WAYS TO USE A DEAD RIVER FLY
        by Bruce Carlson .... paperback $7.95
INDIANA'S VARNISHING OUTHOUSE
        by Bruce Carlson .... paperback $9.95
VACANT LOT, SCHOOL YARD & BACK ALLEY GAMES
        by various authors .... paperback $9.95
HOW TO TALK MIDWESTERN
        by Robert Thomas .... paperback $7.95

IOWA BOOKS

IOWA COOKIN'
        by Bruce Carlson .... (3x5) paperback $5.95
IOWA'S ROADKILL COOKBOOK
        By Bruce Carlson .... paperback $7.95
REVENGE OF ROADKILL
        by Bruce Carlson .... paperback $7.95
IOWA'S OLD SCHOOLHOUSES
        by Carole Turner Johnston .... paperback $9.95
GHOSTS OF THE AMANA COLONIES
        by Lori Erickson .... paperback $9.95
GHOSTS OF THE IOWA GREAT LAKES
        by Bruce Carlson .... paperback $9.95
GHOSTS OF THE MISSISSIPPI RIVER (from Dubuque to Keokuk)
        by Bruce Carlson .... paperback $9.95
GHOSTS OF THE MISSISSIPPI RIVER (from Minneapolis to Dubuque)
        by Bruce Carlson .... paperback $9.95
GHOSTS OF POLK COUNTY, IOWA
        by Tom Welch .... paperback $9.95
TALES OF HACKETT'S CREEK
        by Dan Titus .... paperback $9.95
ME 'N WESLEY (stories about the homemade toys that
    Iowa farm children made and played with around the turn of the century)
        by Bruce Carlson .... paperback $9.95
TALL TALES OF THE MISSISSIPPI RIVER
        by Dan Titus .... paperback $9.95
HOW TO TALK IOWA .... paperback $7.95
UNSOLVED MYSTERIES OF THE MISSISSIPPI
        by Netha Bell .... paperback $9.95
101 WAYS TO USE A DEAD RIVER FLY
        by Bruce Carlson .... paperback $7.95

LET'S US GO DOWN TO THE RIVER 'N...
                by various authors .... paperback $9.95
TRICKS WE PLAYED IN IOWA
                by various authors .... paperback $9.95
IOWA, THE LAND BETWEEN THE VOWELS
    (farm boy stories from the early 1900s)
                by Bruce Carlson .... paperback $9.95
LOST & BURIED TREASURE OF THE MISSISSIPPI RIVER
                by Netha Bell & Gary Scholl .... paperback $9.95
Some Pretty Tame, but Kinda Funny Stories About Early
IOWA LADIES-OF-THE-EVENING
                by Bruce Carlson .... paperback $9.95
THE VANISHING OUTHOUSE OF IOWA
                by Bruce Carlson .... paperback $9.95
IOWA'S EARLY HOME REMEDIES
                by 26 students at Wapello Elem. School .... paperback $9.95
IOWA - A JOURNEY IN A PROMISED LAND
                by Kathy Yoder .... paperback $16.95
LOST & BURIED TREASURE OF THE MISSOURI RIVER
                by Netha Bell .... paperback $9.95
FIELD GUIDE TO IOWA'S CRITTERS
                by Bruce Carlson .... paperback $7.95
OLD IOWA HOUSES, YOUNG LOVES
                by Bruce Carlson .... paperback $9.95
SKUNK RIVER ANTHOLOGY
                by Gene Olson .... paperback $9.95
VACANT LOT, SCHOOL YARD & BACK ALLEY GAMES
                by various authors .... paperback $9.95
HOW TO TALK MIDWESTERN
                by Robert Thomas .... paperback $7.95

KANSAS BOOKS

HOW TO TALK KANSAS .... paperback $7.95
STOPOVER IN KANSAS
                by Jon McAlpin .... paperback $9.95
LET'S US GO DOWN TO THE RIVER 'N ...
                by various authors .... paperback $9.95
LOST & BURIED TREASURE OF THE MISSOURI RIVER
                by Netha Bell .... paperback $9.95

101 WAYS TO USE A DEAD RIVER FLY
        by Bruce Carlson .... paperback $7.95
VACANT LOT, SCHOOL YARD & BACK ALLEY GAMES
        by various authors .... paperback $9.95
HOW TO TALK MIDWESTERN
        by Robert Thomas .... paperback $7.95

KENTUCKY BOOKS

GHOSTS OF THE OHIO RIVER (from Pittsburgh to Cincinnati)
        by Bruce Carlson .... paperback $9.95
GHOSTS OF THE OHIO RIVER (from Cincinnati to Louisville)
        by Bruce Carlson .... paperback $9.95
TALES OF HACKETT'S CREEK
        by Dan Titus .... paperback $9.95
LOST & BURIED TREASURE OF THE MISSISSIPPI RIVER
        by Netha Bell & Gary Scholl .... paperback $9.95
LET'S US GO DOWN TO THE RIVER 'N ...
        by various authors .... paperback $9.95
UNSOLVED MYSTERIES OF THE MISSISSIPPI
        by Netha Bell .... paperback $9.95
101 WAYS TO USE A DEAD RIVER FLY
        by Bruce Carlson .... paperback $7.95
TALL TALES OF THE MISSISSIPPI RIVER
        by Dan Titus .... paperback $9.95
MY VERY FIRST
        by various authors .... paperback $9.95
VACANT LOT, SCHOOL YARD & BACK ALLEY GAMES
        by various authors .... paperback $9.95

MICHIGAN BOOKS

MICHIGAN COOKIN'
        by Bruce Carlson .... (3x5) paperback $5.95
MICHIGAN'S ROADKILL COOKBOOK
        by Bruce Carlson .... paperback $7.95
MICHIGAN'S VANISHING OUTHOUSE
        by Bruce Carlson .... paperback $9.95

MINNESOTA BOOKS

MINNESOTA'S ROADKILL COOKBOOK
      by Bruce Carlson .... paperback $7.95
REVENGE OF ROADKILL
      by Bruce Carlson .... paperback $7.95
A FIELD GUIDE TO SMALL MINNESOTA FEMALES
      by Bruce Carlson .... paperback $9.95
GHOSTS OF THE MISSISSIPPI RIVER (from Minneapolis to Dubuque)
      by Bruce Carlson .... paperback $9.95
LAKES COUNTRY COOKBOOK
      by Bruce Carlson .... paperback $11.95
UNSOLVED MYSTERIES OF THE MISSISSIPPI
      by Netha Bell .... paperback $9.95
TALES OF HACKETT'S CREEK
      by Dan Titus .... paperback $9.95
GHOSTS OF SOUTHWEST MINNESOTA
      by Ruth Hein .... paperback $9.95
HOW TO TALK LIKE A MINNESOTA NATIVE .... paperback $7.95
MINNESOTA'S VANISHING OUTHOUSE
      by Bruce Carlson .... paperback $9.95
TALL TALES OF THE MISSISSIPPI RIVER
      by Dan Titus .... paperback $9.95
Some Pretty Tame, but Kinda Funny Stories About Early
MINNESOTA LADIES-OF-THE-EVENING
      by Bruce Carlson .... paperback $9.95
101 WAYS TO USE A DEAD RIVER FLY .... paperback $7.95
LOST & BURIED TREASURE OF THE MISSISSIPPI RIVER
      by Netha Bell & Gary Scholl .... paperback $9.95
VACANT LOT, SCHOOL YARD & BACK ALLEY GAMES
      by various authors .... paperback $9.95
HOW TO TALK MIDWESTERN
      by Robert Thomas .... paperback $7.95
MINNESOTA COOKIN'
      by Bruce Carlson .... (3x5) paperback $5.95

MISSOURI BOOKS

MISSOURI COOKIN'
      by Bruce Carlson .... (3x5) paperback $5.95
MISSOURI'S ROADKILL COOKBOOK
      by Bruce Carlson .... paperback $7.95

MISSISSIPPI RIVER COOKIN' BOOK
    by Bruce Carlson .... paperback $11.95
MISSOURI'S OLD HOUSES, AND NEW LOVES
    by Bruce Carlson .... paperback $9.95
UNDERGROUND MISSOURI
    by Bruce Carlson .... paperback $9.95

NEBRASKA BOOKS

LOST & BURIED TREASURE OF THE MISSOURI RIVER
    by Netha Bell .... paperback $9.95
101 WAYS TO USE A DEAD RIVER FLY
    by Bruce Carlson .... paperback $7.95
LET'S US GO DOWN TO THE RIVER 'N ...
    by various authors .... paperback $9.95
HOW TO TALK MIDWESTERN
    by Robert Thomas .... paperback $7.95
VACANT LOT, SCHOOL YARD & BACK ALLEY GAMES
    by various authors .... paperback $9.95

TENNESSEE BOOKS

TALES OF HACKETT'S CREED
    by Dan Titus .... paperback $9.95
TALL TALES OF THE MISSISSIPPI RIVER
    by Dan Titus .... paperback $9.95
UNSOLVED MYSTERIES OF THE MISSISSIPPI
    by Netha Bell .... paperback $9.95
LOST & BURIED TREASURE OF THE MISSISSIPPI RIVER
    by Netha Bell & Gary Scholl .... paperback $9.95
LET'S US GO DOWN TO THE RIVER 'N ...
    by various authors .... paperback $9.95
101 WAYS TO USE A DEAD RIVER FLY
    by Bruce Carlson .... paperback $7.95
VACANT LOT, SCHOOL YARD & BACK ALLEY GAMES
    by various authors .... paperback $9.95

WISCONSIN BOOKS

HOW TO TALK WISCONSIN .... paperback $7.95
WISCONSIN COOKIN'
     by Bruce Carlson .... (3x5) paperback $5.95
WISCONSIN'S ROADKILL COOKBOOK
     by Bruce Carlson .... paperback $7.95
REVENGE OF ROADKILL
     by Bruce Carlson .... paperback $7.95
TALL TALES OF THE MISSISSIPPI RIVER
     by Dan Titus .... paperback $9.95
LAKES COUNTRY COOKBOOK
     by Bruce Carlson .... paperback $11.95
TALES OF HACKETT'S CREEK
     by Dan Titus .... paperback $9.95
LET'S US GO DOWN TO THE RIVER 'N ...
     by various authors .... paperback $9.95
101 WAYS TO USE A DEAD RIVER FLY
     by Bruce Carlson .... paperback $7.95
UNSOLVED MYSTERIES OF THE MISSISSIPPI
     by Netha Bell .... paperback $9.95
LOST & BURIED TREASURE OF THE MISSISSIPPI RIVER
     by Netha Bell & Gary Scholl .... paperback $9.95
GHOSTS OF THE MISSISSIPPI RIVER (from Dubuque to Keokuk)
     by Bruce Carlson .... paperback $9.95
HOW TO TALK MIDWESTERN
     by Robert Thomas .... paperback $7.95
VACANT LOT, SCHOOL YARD & BACK ALLEY GAMES
     by various authors .... paperback $9.95
MY VERY FIRST
     by various authors .... paperback $9.95
EARLY WISCONSIN HOME REMEDIES
     by various authors .... paperback $9.95
GHOSTS OF THE MISSISSIPPI RIVER (from Minneapolis to Dubuque)
     by Bruce Carlson .... paperback $9.95
THE VANISHING OUTHOUSE OF WISCONSIN
     by Bruce Carlson .... paperback $9.95
GHOSTS OF DOOR COUNTY, WISCONSIN
     by Geri Rider .... paperback $9.95
Some Pretty Tame, but Kinda Funny Stories About Early
WISCONSIN LADIES-OF-THE-EVENING
     by Bruce Carlson .... paperback $9.95

MIDWESTERN BOOKS

A FIELD GUIDE TO THE MIDWEST'S WORST RESTAURANTS
by Bruce Carlson .... paperback $5.95
THE MOTORIST'S FIELD GUIDE TO MIDWESTERN FARM
EQUIPMENT (misguided information as only a city slicker can give it)
by Bruce Carlson .... paperback $5.95
VACANT LOT, SCHOOL YARD & BACK ALLEY GAMES
OF THE MIDWEST YEARS AGO
by various authors .... paperback $9.95
MIDWEST SMALL TOWN COOKING
by Bruce Carlson .... (3x5) paperback $5.95
HITCHHIKING THE UPPER MIDWEST
by Bruce Carlson .... paperback $7.95
101 WAYS FOR MIDWESTERNERS TO "DO IN" THEIR
NEIGHBOR'S PESKY DOG WITHOUT GETTING CAUGHT
by Bruce Carlson .... paperback $5.95

RIVER BOOKS

ON THE SHOULDERS OF A GIANT
by M. Cody and D. Walker .... paperback $9.95
SKUNK RIVER ANTHOLOGY
by Gene "Will" Olson .... paperback $9.95
JACK KING vs. DETECTIVE MACKENZIE
by Netha Bell .... paperback $9.95
LOST & BURIED TREASURES ALONG THE MISSISSIPPI
by Netha Bell & Gary Scholl .... paperback $9.95
MISSISSIPPI RIVER PO' FOLK
by Pat Wallace .... paperback $9.95
STRANGE FOLKS ALONG THE MISSISSIPPI
by Pat Wallace .... paperback $9.95
GHOSTS OF THE OHIO RIVER (from Pittsburgh to Cincinnati)
by Bruce Carlson .... paperback $9.95
GHOSTS OF THE OHIO RIVER (from Cincinnati to Louisville)
by Bruce Carlson .... paperback $9.95
GHOSTS OF THE MISSISSIPPI RIVER (Minneapolis to Dubuque)
by Bruce Carlson .... paperback $9.95
GHOSTS OF THE MISSISSIPPI RIVER (Dubuque to Keokuk)
by Bruce Carlson .... paperback $9.95
TALL TALES OF THE MISSISSIPPI RIVER
by Dan Titus .... paperback $9.95

TALL TALES OF THE MISSOURI RIVER
        by Dan Titus .... paperback $9.95
RIVER SHARKS & SHENANIGANS
   (tales of riverboat gambling of years ago)
        by Netha Bell .... paperback $9.95
UNSOLVED MYSTERIES OF THE MISSISSIPPI
        by Netha Bell .... paperback $9.95
TALES OF HACKETT'S CREEK (1940s Mississippi River kids)
        by Dan Titus .... paperback $9.95
101 WAYS TO USE A DEAD RIVER FLY
        by Bruce Carlson .... paperback $7.95
LET'S US GO DOWN TO THE RIVER 'N ...
        by various authors .... paperback $9.95
LOST & BURIED TREASURE OF THE MISSOURI
        by Netha Bell .... paperback $9.95

COOKBOOKS

ROARING 20's COOKBOOK
        by Bruce Carlson .... paperback $11.95
DEPRESSION COOKBOOK
        by Bruce Carlson .... paperback $11.95
LAKES COUNTRY COOKBOOK
        by Bruce Carlson .... paperback $11.95
A COOKBOOK FOR THEM WHAT AIN'T DONE A LOT OF COOKIN'
        by Bruce Carlson .... paperback $11.95
FLAT-OUT DIRT-CHEAP COOKIN' COOKBOOK
        by Bruce Carlson .... paperback $11.95
APHRODISIAC COOKING
        by Bruce Carlson .... paperback $11.95
WILD CRITTER COOKBOOK
        by Bruce Carlson .... paperback $11.95
I GOT FUNNIER-THINGS-TO-DO-THAN-COOKIN' COOKBOOK
        by Louise Lum .... paperback $11.95
MISSISSIPPI RIVER COOKIN' BOOK
        by Bruce Carlson .... paperback $11.95
HUNTING IN THE NUDE COOKBOOK
        by Bruce Carlson .... paperback $9.95
DAKOTA COOKIN'
        by Bruce Carlson .... (3x5) paperback $5.95
IOWA COOKIN'
        by Bruce Carlson .... (3x5) paperback $5.95

MICHIGAN COOKIN'
by Bruce Carlson .... (3x5) paperback $5.95
MINNESOTA COOKIN'
by Bruce Carlson .... (3x5) paperback $5.95
MISSOURI COOKIN'
by Bruce Carlson .... (3x5) paperback $5.95
ILLINOIS COOKIN'
by Bruce Carlson .... (3x5) paperback $5.95
WISCONSIN COOKIN'
by Bruce Carlson .... (3x5) paperback $5.95
HILL COUNTRY COOKIN'
by Bruce Carlson .... (3x5) paperback $5.95
MIDWEST SMALL TOWN COOKIN'
by Bruce Carlson .... (3x5) paperback $5.95
APHRODISIAC COOKIN'
by Bruce Carlson .... (3x5) paperback $5.95
PREGNANT LADY COOKIN'
by Bruce Carlson .... (3x5) paperback $5.95
GOOD COOKIN' FROM THE PLAIN PEOPLE
by Bruce Carlson .... (3x5) paperback $5.95
WORKING GIRL COOKING
by Bruce Carlson .... (3x5) paperback $5.95
COOKING FOR ONE
by Barb Layton .... paperback $11.95
SUPER SIMPLE COOKING
by Barb Layton .... (3x5) paperback $5.95
OFF TO COLLEGE COOKBOOK
by Barb Layton .... (3x5) paperback $5.95
COOKING WITH THINGS THAT GO SPLASH
by Bruce Carlson .... (3x5) paperback $5.95
COOKING WITH THINGS THAT GO MOO
by Bruce Carlson .... (3x5) paperback $5.95
COOKING WITH SPIRITS
by Bruce Carlson .... (3x5) paperback $5.95
INDIAN COOKING COOKBOOK
by Bruce Carlson .... paperback $9.95
DIAL-A-DREAM COOKBOOK
by Bruce Carlson .... (3x5) paperback $5.95
HORMONE HELPER COOKBOOK .... (3x5) paperback $5.95

MISCELLANEOUS BOOKS

DEAR TABBY (letters to and from a feline advice columnist)
    by Bruce Carlson .... paperback $5.95
HOW TO BEHAVE (etiquette advice for non-traditional
and awkward circumstances such as attending dogfights,
what to do when your blind date turns out to be your spouse, etc.)
    by Bruce Carlson .... paperback $5.95
REVENGE OF THE ROADKILL
    by Bruce Carlson .... paperback $7.95